HISPANOS

The Palace of the Governors, shown above as it appeared in 1880, was the capitol building under three flags, to 1884, and the place of residence of governors to 1907 (Collections of the School of American Research, in the Museum of New Mexico; photo by Ben Wittick).

HISPANOS
Historic Leaders in New Mexico

By
Lynn I. Perrigo

Sunstone Press
Santa Fe, New Mexico

First Edition

Printed in the United States of America

Library of Congress Cataloging in Publication Data:

Perrigo, Lynn I., 1903
    Hispanos: historic leaders in New Mexico.

    Includes index.
    1. Hispanic Americans--New Mexico--Biography. 2. New
Mexico--Biography. I. Title.
F805.S75P47   1985   978.9'00468 [B]   85-489
ISBN: 0-86534-011-0

Published in 1985 by SUNSTONE PRESS
                Post Office Box 2321
                Santa Fe, NM 87504-2321 / USA

CONTENTS

PREFACE

The evolution of New Mexico has been well described in several state and regional histories. In them, after the Spanish and Mexican periods, the emphasis is upon the "westernizing" process, that is, the flurry of activity by newcomers in the transformation that occurred as the area was being developed into an integral part of the United States.

The purpose of this book is to present a sampling of the careers of eminent Hispanos so that an appraisal of that part of the story can be made more readily. When done, it is noteworthy that much of the history of New Mexico, the "Land of Enchantment," is interwoven in the experiences of the several subjects.

A bibliography of all sources drawn upon for detail and background would fill much space. Nevertheless, I am obligated at least to give credit to a few works, each of which provided information about several of the individuals. They are Gilberto Espinosa and Tibo V. Chávez, *El Río Abajo*, edited by Carter M. Waid; Ralph Emerson Twitchell, *The Leading Facts of New Mexico History*; Maurilio E. Vigil, *Los Patrones: Profiles of Hispanic Political Leaders in New Mexico*; Nancy Benson, *Notable Women of New Mexico*; State Planning Office, *The Historic Preservation Program in New Mexico, Volume II*; and various works by Fray Angélico Chávez and Father Stanley Crocchiola. In addition, I must admit that I have condensed some passages from one of my books, *The American Southwest*.

To three specialists in this field, now associated with New Mexico Highlands University, I am indebted for their critical reading of the manuscript and their appraisal of its contents. They are Dr. Guillermo Lux, Professor of History; Dr. Maurilio E. Vigil, Professor of Political Science, and Dr. John A. Aragón, President.

In addition, Arthur Olivas, Photographic Archivist, Museum of New Mexico, Lane Ittleson, Deputy Historic Preservation Officer, and Richard Salazar, Deputy Director, State Records Center, lent assistance with the procurement of photographs for illustrations.

Although the term "Hispanos" has come into widespread use only recently, it has been employed in the title because it is current and comprehensive. Through much of the time encompassed by this series of profiles, Anglos commonly referred to the Spanish-speaking people as "Spanish Americans" and "Mexicans," whereas the latter usually called themselves *Neo-Mejicanos* and *Hispano-Americanos*. In this work, therefore, "Hispanos" and "Spanish Americans" are used interchangeably. The term "Mexican Americans" generally has been inapplicable throughout the history of this state, because there have been but few recent migrants having a heritage of rural Mexican folk culture. There is one in this series of biographical sketches who might then have been so regarded, because he was born in Mexico; but, as will be seen later, he soon became a close affiliate of the people descended from pioneers having a more direct Spanish heritage.

As a rule, whenever there is an appropriate noun, as, *Hispanos*, the adjective, *Hispanics*, need not be employed as a noun. However, early in the course of popularization of that term, writers for the media introduced the improper usage, and others have repeated it until it has become commonplace. That does not justify a deviation from the preferable practice in the title and context of this formal study.

Lynn I. Perrigo

While Juan de Oñate was traveling afar in his futile quest of a great discovery, he had the above inscription engraved at El Morro (Museum of New Mexico).

I   First on the Frontier

After Spanish exploration of the northern frontier of New Spain between 1528 and 1541 a recess of over half of a century followed, and there was a reason for it. A search for wealth was the main motive of that era, and no great riches had been found.

In succeeding years Spaniards became inspired by new motives. For one, in 1542 a debate between Franciscan friars and would-be conquerors was settled by a royal decree in support of the contention of the friars that the Indians in America were human beings who had souls to be saved instead of something akin to animals subject to enslavement. That introduced two new motives — conversion and the colonization necessary to effect it and to develop the frontier. Then, as more time passed, the opening of silver mines north of Mexico City and wars with Indians pushed the frontier northward into Chihuahua, where a shorter route was found to New Mexico, up the Río Grande instead of over the mountains from western Mexico and thence across what now is Arizona. This revived interest in the land of "The Seven Cities."

In that era the Crown let contracts to the highest bidder, that is, to the nobleman who had a favorable ancestral record and who offered to put the most resources into a colonizing expedition. In 1595 Juan de Oñate won the contract for colonizing New Mexico. His father, who had come to New Spain in 1541, was a veteran of the Indian wars who had acquired wealth from mining. Moreover, Oñate was a personal friend of the viceroy, and his wife had a dowry as a descendant of Hernando Córtez, the conqueror of Mexico City.

That this definitely was to be a colonizing expedition is evident in Oñate's offer to enlist 200 men, some with families, for that purpose "by peaceful means, friendliness, and Christian zeal," as well as by the supplies he proposed to take along. They included 500 *pesos'* worth of cattle, as well as a great variety of tools. However, he requested that the king support the six friars who would accompany him for conversion of the Indians. For himself he asked for an annual salary, for the title of *marquis*, and for the right to select thirty square leagues of land, including his jurisdiction over "all of the subjects who may live within the said territory." His captains would be given titles as *hidalgos* (gentlemen) and the right to make vassals of many Indians under a system then known as *encomienda*.

Ultimately the latter would contribute one of the causes of the Pueblo Rebellion of 1680.

When Oñate had made the promised preparations by 1595, a new unfriendly viceroy and the ambition of a rival nobleman caused a delay of three years, and in that time Oñate's 200 followers became discouraged and dwindled down to 129. The tribulations of that interval are related in intimately revealing documents translated by Agapito Rey and edited by George P. Hammond. Finally, in 1598, after Oñate's authorization definitely had been reaffirmed, the viceroy's inspector gave consent for the expedition to proceed, upon securing Oñate's pledge that he would enlist 80 colonists to follow later as substitutes for those who had deserted.

When the procession arrived at the Río Grande, Oñate conducted a ceremony by which he claimed possession of all "lands, pueblos, cities, towns, castles, fortified and unfortified houses which now are established in the kingdoms of and provinces of New Mexico,...the mountains, rivers, fisheries, waters, pastures, valleys, meadows, springs, and ores of gold, silver, copper, mercury, tin, iron, precious stones, [and] salt..."

As the expedition passed through one pueblo after another, Oñate cajoled the occupants into peaceable submission. Finally, on July 11, a vanguard chose the site of the Pueblo of Ohke near the confluence of the Río Grande and the Chama River for a settlement to be called *San Juan Bautista*. When the main expedition arrived there on August 18, the colonists built a church and shelters for their families. A year later they moved from the pueblo to a site on the west side of the Río Grande, which they named *San Gabriel*.

Soon an inconsistency fomented discontent. The colonists had come to make homes, and the friars to convert Indians. Oñate had held out those prospects; but upon his arrival he became obsessed with the out-of-date motive of his predecessors — to find great wealth for himself, his captains, and the Crown, or else to make a discovery which would redound to his credit. To that end he sent a company on a journey into what is now Arizona, where the captain thought that he found a rich mine. He sent another to subdue cruelly the the rebellious Indians of the "Sky City" of Ácoma. Next, in 1601, he led a fruitless expedition of 70 soldiers east past the Pecos Pueblo and out onto the buffalo plains.

As the colonists and friars became discontented due to the stringencies of this frontier and the almost constant absence of their leader, many of them returned to New Spain. Aware that they would make unfavorable reports about his administration, Oñate gambled upon one more desperate attempt to find something that would bring him great glory. On this final journey he led about thirty soldiers far westward to the Colorado River and the Gulf of California.

Upon his return, empty-handed, bad news awaited him. The Council of the Indies had ordered an investigation, whereupon Oñate resigned. At this critical juncture the Council even considered abandoning New Mexico, because it was "hopeless"; but the plea of a friar in behalf of an exaggerated thousands of Indians, whom he claimed had been converted, led to a decision to continue the settlement as a royal colony for missionary purposes rather than as the personal domain of a nobleman. A new governor, Pedro de Peralta, who relieved Oñate in the autumn of 1609, soon moved the colonists to a new site at Santa Fe, where they would be farther removed from Indian pueblos.

The feeble colony survived through subsequent vicissitudes, with the exception of the Pueblo Rebellion of 1680, which forced the survivors to flee to El Paso del Norte. Because they returned later, the colony actually had continuity on through to better times.

As for Oñate, a trial begun in 1612 led to his conviction for engaging in immoral conduct, for resorting to severe treatment of Indians, for exaggerating the riches of New Mexico, and for mistreating his officers. The penalties were loss of his titles, banishment from Mexico City for four years, and a fine of 6,000 ducats.

If Oñate had not got his motives crossed up, he might have continued his residence in New Mexico and could have attained even greater eminence. As it was, he suffered dearly for making a small beginning of what turned out later to be a great achievement — the founding in New Mexico of a permanent colony that antedated both Jamestown in Virginia and Plymouth in Massachusetts.

After the devastating Pueblo Rebellion of 1680, Diego de Vargas led a peaceful entrada to Santa Fe followed by a forceful reconquest (Museum of New Mexico).

II   Revenge for Rebellion

New Mexico was all but abandoned by its Spanish settlers 300 years ago as the result of a destructive rebellion by the Pueblo Indians. It was not abandoned entirely, because the colonists fled to Isleta, near present El Paso del Norte, where they awaited an opportunity to return to their former homeland in the upper valley of the Rio Grande.

After an attempted reconquest had failed, a new governor came to El Paso. He was Don Diego de Vargas, a descendant of an illustrious family in Madrid and married to a lady of another distinguished Spanish family. Although he possessed a vast estate of lands and mansions in Spain and New Spain, he was burdened with indebtedness. In New Mexico he would seek, without success a financial recovery. As summed up by John L. Kessell in an article in the *New Mexico Historical Review*, he was "a loving and lonely family man cursed all of his life by reduced circumstances."

First, in 1692, to make the headquarters in El Paso secure, Vargas mustered the soldiers and chased away the hostile Indians in that vicinity. Next, in August of that same year, he ventured northward with about 200 men and met no opposition until he came to Santa Fe. There he laid siege to the town, which was swarming with Indians. After he had cut off their supply of water in the town ditch, they surrendered.

He absolved those natives of their heresy and then marched his men from one pueblo to another. In short order he regained control over 23 pueblos, at least superficially, without any bloodshed excepting that incurred in skirmishes with Apaches.

Back in El Paso a year later the colonists prepared for the journey to their devastated homeland. With appropriate ceremony 70 families set forth in October, 1693, accompanied by 100 soldiers, 18 Franciscan friars, and many Indian allies and servants.

This time several of the pueblos prepared to resist, because they feared that Vargas would not keep his promise of forgiveness. In December Vargas tried for two weeks to negotiate with the chiefs of the Indians who occupied Santa Fe. Because 21 of the colonists died from exposure while camping out in the cold, Vargas ordered his soldiers to batter down the gates of the town. That done, the Spaniards occupied the *villa* with the loss of only one life. Then the soldiers lined up 70 of the Indian leaders, had a friar say a prayer for them, and executed them.

In early 1694 the colonists and soldiers were settled in Santa Fe, but only three outlying pueblos were friendly. Vargas promptly subdued the others in a rapid series of marches and assaults. Once more Spanish settlement spread out in the vicinity of the capital.

Another revolt occurred in June, 1696, when six of the pueblos arose with renewed fury and killed five friars and 21 colonists. Again Vargas raged up and down the valley, battering down resistance with a vengeance.

He thought that he had earned reappointment as governor, but due to false allegations about him by jealous rivals, a new governor, Pedro Rodríguez Cubero, arrived in 1697 to take his place. He conducted a mock trial, found Vargas guilty of all kinds of wrong doing, seized his property, and ordered him locked in jail for an indefinite term.

After a friend had persuaded authorities in Mexico City that an injustice had been done, an order was sent out for the release of Vargas and his reappointment, whereupon Cubero hastily fled to Mexico. Again the determined governor departed on another campaign against hostile Indians, this time the Apaches; but his health had been undermined by his three years in jail. He died at Bernalillo on April 8, 1704.

Although the Spaniards had grown weary of having their men called from their homes so much of the time for military campaigns, finally they did come to an appreciation of what this resolute conqueror had accomplished. He is reputed to have conducted a peaceable *entrada*, and he did the first time; but later it turned into bloody warfare. By sheer force he had made the colony secure for some time to come. He also had fostered future peace by abolishing the *encomienda* system by which Spaniards previously had exacted exploitive tribute from the Indians consigned to them. Finally, this relentless leader had sacrificed his own life for the welfare of his subjects in that remote colony.

(Note: The writing of "De Vargas" has become a common practice, but the inclusion of the preposition is French usage, as, "De Smet," whereas in Spanish the names are alphabetized by the nouns, as "Oñate," not "De Oñate." The authoritative Spanish historian, Darío Fernández Flores, wrote "Vargas," and so did the leading contemporary historian of New Spain's northern frontier, the Reverend John Francis Bannon.)

III   Across the Southwest

In Spanish times the governors sent to New Mexico typically stayed only a few years and in that time sought by all means to gain wealth as the result of that appointment. A notable exception was Juan Bautista de Anza, who stayed for ten years and seriously sought to improve the status of the colony. Previously he had rendered outstanding services in Arizona, and altogether his achievements earned for him recognition as the greatest frontiersman of his era.

Anza was born on the frontier in Sonora, where his father and grandfather had been loyal servants of the Spanish government. He, too, enlisted for military service in 1752 at the age of 17, and 22 years later, at a critical time on the northern frontier, he was captain of the soldiers posted in the *presidio* of Tubac in a region then know as *Pimería Alta*, now southern Arizona. On the frontier were three other unconnected Spanish outposts, in Texas, in New Mexico, and in California. Their security was threatened not only by Indians but also by the movement of Russians down the Pacific coast from their base in Alaska, by the approach of French fur traders from their colony in Canada, and by the advance of English settlers from the east coast toward the Mississippi River in territory wrested from France in 1763.

Because vigorous Spanish action was needed, the frontier was designated as a military department, to which an able commander, Teodoro de Croix, was assigned in 1777. He determined to build a line of forts all across the borderlands, to strengthen the militia, and to make an alliance with one of the stronger of the Indian tribes, the Comanche, in order to have their aid in the defense of Texas and New Mexico against other Indians and the Europeans.

Previously Anza had come up with another idea. He believed that by opening an overland route from Tubac to California, supplies could be transported to the feebly sustained missions there by it better than by the hazardous journey in ships up the west coast. When he made that proposal in Mexico City, the viceroy granted approval for him to lead twenty volunteers from Tubac on a trip west to explore such a route, with the much-traveled Padre Francisco Garcés as his guide.

Anza and his party departed from Tubac in January, 1774, made a pause in the journey to win the friendship of the Yuma Indians,

15

who controlled the best place for a crossing of the Colorado river, arrived in San Diego in March, and returned to Tubac late in May. When Anza described to the viceroy his successful opening of a trail, that official promoted him to the rank of lieutenant colonel and authorized him to lead a colonizing expedition to California for the strengthening of the support of the Franciscan missions there and for heading off Russian aggression.

Forthwith Anza gathered together 240 persons at Tubac and prepared them for the journey to California. This expedition, the best organized of any in the history of New Spain, made the long trip expeditiously and safely and in March, 1776, founded a colony which later became San Francisco.

For his distinguished service Anza was rewarded in 1778 with an appointment as governor of New Mexico. That turned out to be less of a reward and more of a duty to try to carry out the plan of Croix for enlisting as allies the Comanches, who were described as "superb horsemen" and "magnificent warriors," but the major obstacle would be a belligerent band of them led by their wily chief, Cuerno Verdo. If he could be eliminated, the other bands might be brought in for a conference.

In August, 1779, Anza assembled at Taos soldiers, settlers, and Indian allies to the total number of 573, and for those who were ill-equipped, he provided horses and guns. As described in documents translated by Alfred Barnaby Thomas, he marched the army northward into the Colorado mountains and then veered to the east onto the high plains, where he picked up the trail of the Comanches and overtook them near the Arkansas River. In the battle that ensued, the Spaniards killed Cuerno Verde, one of his sons, and four of his captains, as well as many of the warriors.

While awaiting the effects of that victory, Anza turned his attention to Arizona. After he had departed from the *presidio* which he had founded at Tucsón, soldiers posted among the Yumas at the crossing place of the Colorado River mistreated those Indians, who massacred them in 1780 and closed that route to California. Since Arizona then lost its importance as a half-way house on the former route, the defenses were neglected there and Apaches threatened extinction of that small colony. In consequence, in 1780 Anza led an expedition into Arizona to frighten away those Apaches. That brought relief to the few settlers there and encouraged expansion of that colony.

Next, as news of the strength of the Spaniards under their able

Shown above are the ruins of the Pecos Pueblo and Mission, where Anza once made a treaty of peace with an assemblage of Comanche Chiefs (Historic Preservation Bureau; photo by Fred Mang, Jr.).

commander spread among the Comanches, over 400 of them came to Taos in 1785 to talk peace, but Anza refused to deal with them unless all bands were represented. Then they called together numerous groups for a council about that, and nearly all lodges sent representatives to Pecos for a conference with the governor and his aides. There terms of peace and commerce finally were agreed upon.

After Diego de Vargas had pacified the Pueblo Indians, almost constant troubles with Comanches and Apaches had been the major threat to the settlements in New Mexico, and afterwards some of the Apaches had found that trading was more profitable than raiding. That left the Comanches as the principal danger to be dealt with, and if won over, they could be counted upon to help hold off other unfriendly Apaches and the hostile Utes. Finally the courageous, persistent efforts of Governor Anza had contributed what was needed most for encouragement of growth and prosperity through many years after his death in 1788.

In commemoration of Anza's services imaginative villagers revised a Spanish folkplay and renamed it *Los Comanches*. In it men acting the part of Indians under Cuerno Verde and others representing Spanish soldiers under Anza engaged in spectacular maneuvers until finally in battle Anza emerged victorious. In that manner their hero's most significant achievement was reenacted dramatically year after year for long afterward by the appreciative citizens of New Mexico.

IV   Emissary to Spain

In the decade beginning in 1810 concerned citizens in Santa Fe received thought-provoking news, as a democratic spirit mounted in both Spain and New Spain. In the latter, the colony in which New Mexico was a province, the agitation grew into an outright rebellion which finally gained independence from Spain and created the Mexican nation in 1821.

In Spain the proponents of change pursued a different course. They deposed their weak emperor, Charles IV, who was succeeded by his son, Ferdinand VII; but soon Napoleon Bonaparte directed a French invasion, and occupation, of the peninsula and replaced Ferdinand with his brother Joseph Bonaparte. Then Spanish liberals, meeting in Cádiz in 1810, called for delegates to assemble there as a *cortes*, or parliament, for drafting a constitution under which that body would become the legislative assembly in a constitutional monarchy. They would still have an emperor, but would have a democratic assembly share in his powers in law-making.

Since the colonies were to have representation in the Cortes, the call went out even to distant Santa Fe. There nearly all of the *alcaldes* in New Mexico met on August 11, 1810, to select a delegate. From among three candidates they chose Pedro Bautista Pino, whom Ralph Emerson Twitchell described later as "the most able statesman ever born in New Mexico during Spanish rule." He was a wealthy, well-educated, highly respected *don*, who was descended from two pioneers who had come to Santa Fe with Diego de Vargas. His wife, Ana María, also could trace her ancestry back to another arrival at that time, whose name illustrates the interesting custom of recognizing several contributors to a distinguished lineage. That captains's full name was Nicolás Órtiz Niño Ladrón de Guevara.

Because a long journey overland to Vera Cruz and by ship to Spain lay ahead of the selected delegate, he concluded that immediate departure would require that he pay his own expenses and those of his nephew, who would accompany him. The citizens of Santa Fe did hastily raise about 5,000 *pesos*, not for his expenses but for him to present as a gift to the emperor.

On August 5, 1812, the two travelers arrived in Cádiz, and Don Pedro joined in the deliberations of the Cortes, which already had completed the drafting of a constitution five months previously.

His contribution, therefore, was limited to a presentation of his plea in behalf of his fellow New Mexicans, which he had had a friend write and had entitled as his *Exposición*. In it he petitioned for a reorganization of the colonial military establishment, the founding of five more *presidios*, or forts, salaries for men serving in the militia, a bishopric for New Mexico separate from that of Durango, and support for a system of schools.

He departed soon afterward for a visit in London, fortunately, because when Ferdinand VII returned to the throne in 1814, he dissolved the Cortes, abrogated the Constitution, and clapped in jail liberal leaders, including the delegates from Mexico. That restored, reactionary emperor ignored the requests of Pino as presented in his *Exposición*.

After an absence of three years Don Pedro and his nephew returned from the longest voyage made by any citizen of Santa Fe in the colonial period. The reception was cordial, even exciting, as the townsmen were eager to hear his recounting of his experiences and especially eager to see the new, luxurious carriage which he had purchased in London for shipment all of the way to Santa Fe. As for his meagre accomplishments, they summed them up tersely in a popular saying that he went and returned. *Don Pedro Pino fué, y Don Pedro Pino vino.*

The real effects followed later. The ignoring of Pino's requests was taken as another evidence, among many, of Spanish neglect of the colonists in remote New Mexico. As a result, when news arrived that Mexico had won independence, the residents of Santa Fe hopefully celebrated that event on January 6, 1822, by conducting joyous parades, followed by a *baile* that night in the Palace of the Governors. Further, after Don Pedro's *Exposición* was translated into English, and published, it became a valuable source for historical studies of conditions in New Mexico immediately prior to the dawning of the Mexican Period in 1821.

V   The Favored Family

The current telephone directory for Santa Fe has 415 listings of the name of Martínez, 337 of Romero, 324 of Gonzales and González, 251 of Montoya, 213 of Órtiz, 208 of Roybal, 194 of Trujillo, 186 of Baca and C. de Baca, 183 of Vigil, 177 of García, 165 of Chávez, 154 of López, 136 of Sánchez, 128 of Gallegos, 127 of Sandoval, 126 of Luján, 121 of Rodríguez, 118 of Rivera, 114 of Valdes and Váldez, 104 of Quintana, and between 20 and 100 of several other Spanish names, as against 112 Smiths, 81 Johnsons, and 75 Joneses.

The origins of most of the Hispanic families can be traced back to one or more of those respective names listed by Fray Angélico Chávez in his books about the pioneers who migrated from Spain and from New Spain to New Mexico long ago. The one selected here as an eminent illustration is Luis María C. de Baca, because information about him and his origin is available in several other sources.

Back in 1212 A.D., when Spaniards were driving out the Moors, Martín Alhaja guided soldiers through a mountain pass by marking it with the skull of a cow set on a stake. For that service the king of Navarre knighted him and gave him the name Cabeza de Vaca (Or Baca, The Head of a Cow.) His descendants, favored by the royalty, became noted in their service to Spain, and many became wealthy.

One of his descendants, Álvar Núñez Cabeza de Baca, sailed to Florida in 1528 as treasurer of the ill-fated Narváez expedition. After suffering defeat by Indians, the 250 Spaniards tried to sail on rafts around the gulf to New Spain, now Mexico, only to be shipwrecked in a storm off of the coast of Texas. Núñez and three other survivors, including Estevan, the first black man to see the Southwest, traveled slowly across Texas, across southern New Mexico and Arizona, and down into New Spain.

Afterward Núñez described his journey in a book which stimulated much migration to New Spain and to New Mexico by others, including C. de Bacas and some whose names had been abbreviated to Baca. Incidentally, by Spanish custom a mother's name was added to that of her husband for one generation, and the continuing, paternal surname was what would appear to Anglos as a middle name, in this case, Núñez. However, if the mother were of a distinguished family, sometimes the offspring chose to perpetuate the name of that illustrious lineage, and that became the practice of the C. de Bacas.

A family of them joined with others in founding Peña Blanca in about 1670, and by 1803 Luis María C. de Baca emerged as an influential man in that village. In 1815 he decided to take advantage of the favoritism enjoyed by the C. de Bacas by applying for a large land grant at Jémez — one which had been abandoned by Antonio Órtiz due to harassment by Indians. After Don Luis had erected buildings and had moved his family and livestock there, he, too, had to abandon that site.

As Don Luis went forth in search of another location, he visited San Miguel del Bado, where a resident, who had grazed sheep in the valley of the Gallinas River, showed him the lush meadows there, and Don Luis decided that that was the place for him. In 1821 his application for a mammoth ranch of close to 500,000 acres was approved, and then he built a house at Las Vegas and moved there his family and 600 mules and horses, as related by Father Stanley.

Losses to Indians caused the C. de Bacas to return to Peña Blanca, but Don Luis tried the new site again in 1826, only briefly, because a year later he was back in Peña Blanca again. Then when the Young-Sublette party of trappers came by, they left in his care several bundles of furs. Mexican soldiers, who found that cache in 1828, claimed that the furs had been trapped illicitly, because Don Luis did not have a license from the governor, Manuel Armijo. The outcome of the ensuing quarrel was that the soldiers shot and killed Don Luis and confiscated the furs.

When Josiah Gregg traveled the Santa Fe Trail across the Meadows in 1833, he found residing there a Mexican *ranchero*, who may have been a sheepherder from San Miguel, or perhaps one of the sons of Don Luis. However, the site soon became unoccupied; therefore the *Diputación* in Santa Fe granted the large former C. de Baca tract to applicants in San Miguel del Bado in 1835, and they founded the town of Las Vegas.

By three wives in succession Don Luis had 23 children. Ralph Emerson Twitchell listed the names of all of them and those of his 88 grandchildren. This C. de Baca family, like that of many other *dons*, multiplied prolifically. Five of those Bacas who moved to Las Vegas were wealthy, built fine homes, and had numerous progeny.

When it came time for the claimants to file for the confirmation of their land grants by the United States, three citizens of Las Vegas made application for the large community land grant there in behalf of themselves and others, and the C. de Baca heirs employed a Santa Fe attorney, John S. Watts, to make application for the same tract in their behalf. Because both claims seemed to be valid, the Congress disposed of the C. de Baca heirs by authorizing Watts to select for them five tracts of 100,000 acres each at other locations which were unoccupied, and then confirmed title to the Las Vegas Grant to the community of Las Vegas. The C. de Baca heirs paid Watts his fee of $3,000 by giving him their "Baca Location," or "Baca Float," in Colorado, and later he sold it for $40,000.

This sketch has presented briefly the experiences of one wealthy *don* who acquired a vast acreage for inheritance by his numerous descendants.

VI   A Typical Don Juan

The title of *don* was employed as an indication of respect for an important person. The qualifications usually were a senior position in the extended family group, ownership of property, and attainment of literacy. Those traits, especially the latter, often brought to a *don* another attribute — an appointment to a minor or major office in government. When used correctly, the title was combined with only the given name, but many deviated from that practice.

The *don* singled out herein as typical of many others is Juan Gerónimo Torres of El Sabinal, a village located on *El Camino Real* south of Belén. In 1850, the year following the death of Don Juan, it had a population of about 600 persons.

The evidence about this *don* affirms that not all of them were extremely wealthy. He owned a tract of forty acres in El Sabinal and another field of about the same size in Belén. His livestock included ninety-one cattle, eighteen goats, eleven oxen, and eleven horses. For care of the animals and cultivation of crops he could call upon eight male servants, who resided in seven cottages which were appraised at 21 *pesos* altogether, and an inventory made in 1849 revealed that each owed Don Juan an average of 30 *pesos*. In other words, they were bound to him in a status of debt servitude. Incidentally, at that time a goat was valued at one *peso* and a horse at eight *pesos*.

Señor Torres, his *doña*, and their five children resided in a nine room house built around a *patio*. Back of it was a woodlot, a vineyard, and an orchard, all surrounded by an adobe wall. In addition, at the time of his death in 1849 five of his acquaintances owed him a total of almost 1,400 *pesos*. The value of all of his assets amounted to a little over 3,000 *pesos*, which would be the equivalent of about $60,000 dollars in modern currency.

Typical of many *dons*, he held an appointment as deputy *alcalde*, in his case from 1821 to 1827 and again in the 1830s. He was atypical, however, in that he preserved carefully his official documents, which have been handed down in the Torres family in Socorro. They afford revealing glimpses into his personal affairs and into the legal milieu in which he functioned.

Once a rival, another Torres, in the presence of others had called him a *revolucionario*, or, in modern lingo, a subversive person. This so infuriated Don Juan that he requested the governor to order his accuser to prove his charges before a "public hearing by an impartial tribunal." Apparently that ended this controversy, because no record of a hearing was preserved in his papers.

The documents include a compilation of statutes sent out from Santa Fe in 1826. If the ditch *mayordomo* neglected his responsibilities, he was to be fined three *pesos*, and if someone appropriated for his own use water turned into the ditch for somebody else, the penalty would be one *peso*. Similar fines were imposed for allowing cattle to damage a neighbor's crops, for polluting the springs reserved for household use, for disobeying a request to contribute labor on the ditches, roads, and church, for failure to respond to the call when the militia went forth in pursuit of enemies, for getting caught at gambling or operating a gambling table, and even for making insulting remarks to others.

Especially strict were the requirements for collection of tithes for the church. The collector had to keep a list of all animals and observe the fields being cultivated in order not to miss anything. From each parishioner he was to exact one of every ten parts, without allowing anyone "to deduct the cost of the seed, rent, or any other expense, nor to pay any debt."

The paternal diligence of the adult population is evident in one revealing statute which reads even more poetic in the original Spanish script than in this writer's translation of it:

It is evident that the author of nature has not imposed the silence of the night with any other object than sleep and rest for living things, and even if some transgressions invert this custom in order thereby to engage in diversions and authorized social companionship, since here we lack such things, it may be clearly inferred that anyone who goes forth through the plazas and fields after nine at night henceforth must be held in detention until the following day and assessed one *peso* fine.

When Don Juan died in 1849, in his *testamento* was a request that he be interred in a robe of the Order of St. Francis. That meant that he had taken a vow to observe the rules of the Third Order, which was an organization sponsored by the Franciscans for enlisting support of prominent laymen in their missionary work.

(Note: Anyone who is interested can find my translation of all of the documents, in full, in the New Mexico Historical Review, April and July, 1951, and January, 1952. They were made available to me by Edward E. Torres of Socorro — L.P.)

VII   The Ghost Town

At old San Miguel del Bado little remains today besides the beautiful, massive church, built in 1806. In the 1830s that community, near present Ribera, was thriving as the port of entry on the Santa Fe Trail, as the seat of Mexican government for the district east of the mountains, and as the place of residence of over 2,000 people.

Juan de Dios Maese was one of four prominent citizens of San Miguel who had the foresight to seek a new place for a settlement, because their town was becoming overcrowded. They chose a location on the meadows in the valley of the Gallinas River, where their application for the Las Vegas community land grant was approved by the *Diputación* in Santa Fe in 1835. They and thirty-three others then moved to that site. There Maese, like the others, obtained a strip of land fronting upon the river and extending westward to *la acequia*.

In that new community he was selected to serve as the *alcalde*. That placed upon him great responsibility, because at that remote location he received very little help from Santa Fe. He was the government for seventeen years. His duties were typical of *alcaldes*. They included supervising volunteer labor on the ditches, roads, and church, maintaining defense against Indians, granting strips of land to newcomers, and managing legal affairs. For the latter the *alcaldes* received part of the fees that they exacted for their attesting to legal documents. He prospered, as evidenced by the fact that presently he was able to build a grist mill.

When *Los Americanos* took over in August, 1846, Maese entered upon troublous times. As the villagers were overawed by the numbers, and the cannon, of the Army of the West, General Stephen Watts Kearny ordered him to climb a ladder, with Kearny, to the roof of a residential building and take the oath of new allegiance before 150 men of Las Vegas, who had assembled in the Plaza.

After the army had marched on to Santa Fe and thence to California, the uprisings in Taos and Mora created unrest in Las Vegas. Once Maese called a meeting at which he sought to calm down the townsmen. Later, he warned that trouble was imminent and was suspected of having abandoned his quest for peace. Therefore, as harassment of ranchers in the vicinity became

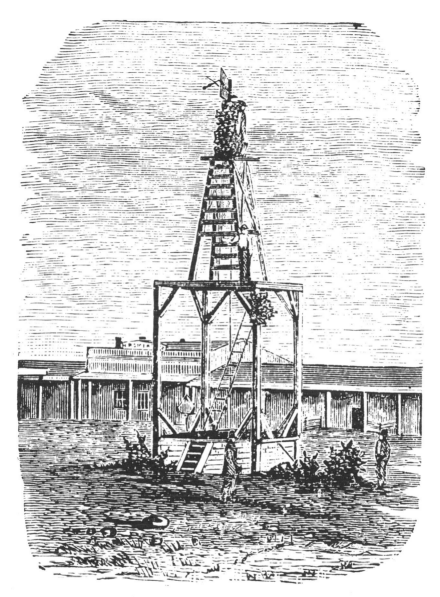

"Hanging Windmill" Plaza, Las Vegas, New Mexico, ca. 1879.

serious, the detachment of cavalry posted near Las Vegas arrested about 50 suspects, including the *alcalde*, whose mill they burned down. However, in a trial in Santa Fe in August, 1847, he was exonerated, along with all but six of the others who were hanged. Finally, in 1852, when San Miguel County was organized, with the county seat at first in San Miguel del Bado, Maese must have been relieved to be shed of the duties of governing.

One can only surmise as to the motives of this former *alcalde* in founding another settlement. Perhaps it was because he had been humiliated, and his property destroyed, by the newcomers. Maybe he felt that Las Vegas had become too crowded and too unruly. (In 1874 a newspaper in Santa Fe published the allegation that Las Vegas had become the "most disorderly place in the territory.") Or, possibly because once he had been successful in founding a new colony, he was confident that he could do it again and find serenity at a location more remote.

At any rate, in 1870 he and others moved to a site rather far away, in the valley of the lower Gallinas River. There they founded a village which they named *La Liendre*. For a time it was successful. By 1880 the population had grown to 388, and on past 1920 it remained above 300; but by 1940 it had declined to 105, and thenceforth it faded out fast until only a ghost town remains today.

When interviewed in 1955, the grandson of the former *alcalde*, Ramón Maes, described life in La Liendre in its heyday. He told about the houses they built, the crops they raised, the work the women did, the school and church they maintained, and, above all, about the peaceable, friendly, orderly community they sustained.

Unfortunately, those villagers, lacking knowledge of the required procedures, and lacking familiarity with the English language, neglected to file for water rights, so that as consumption increased upstream, their ditches dried up even before the Cartwright court decision gave precedence in rights to the City of Las Vegas. Ramón Maes lamented that, "without water our village could not live."

As a leader in colonization Juan de Dios Maese had been successful the first time but disappointed in the later turn of affairs. He was successful again the second time, but ultimately that effort was doomed to complete failure. Because at least some sketchy information about him is available, he has been singled out here as typifying the leaders in many such adventures in colonization by unsung heroes of early times in New Mexico.

VIII   Life on the Frontier

Man and wife, they toiled together in founding this or that colony in mountain valleys or in the foothills of the Sangre de Cristos. This description of their role is a composite of observations by early visitors and reminiscences of old-timers.

They had departed from familiar people and familiar surroundings in either Mexico or the valley of the Río Grande, and either one was very far away by the means for travel in those days. They had left a homeland behind, perhaps forever, in their quest of a new opportunity on a parcel of good land in a new, less crowded community.

It has been said that the Puritans introduced the "work ethic" in America, but nobody else worked harder than this nameless couple. The man arose before daybreak to tend the livestock and then to work seasonally all day in his *milpa* near at hand, with primitive tools which he made himself. He sent sons and their dogs up into a mountain valley for the lonely task of keeping watch over a flock of sheep which he had obtained from a *don* under the *partido*, or share, system. When called upon by the *mayordomo*, he had to join with others in their work on the common ditches and roads, as well as for trips in oxcarts to shovel up loads of salt in distant *salinas* and for forays on horseback far out onto the plains in a hunt for buffalo. Besides, he built his own house and barn of materials at hand and made what furniture the family had. Moreover, he responded to the plea of the priest to help with the building, and care, of the village church, where all worshipped on Sundays and on other holy days. To all of this has to be added those times when this Minute Man had to protect his home and family and village from harassment by unfriendly Indians.

The woman, too, arose before daybreak to prepare breakfast for the family. Then she worked all day, processing foods for other meals and carding, spinning, weaving, and sewing while making all of the clothing for the family. Out in the garden she labored seasonally herself and at supervision of the children while all raised, tended, harvested, and dried the vegetables sorely needed for subsistence. In addition she was the teacher for the children in their learning of Spanish, of traditions, of religion, and of household crafts. That was not all, because whenever some were ill, she was their physician, who knew what herb was best for the treatment of

Many pioneers became skillful in handcrafting their furnishings and tools, as evidenced by exhibits in the State Museum (Historic Preservation Bureau, from the Tourist Bureau).

each kind of sickness and what precaution must be taken to drive away the evil spirit. In between, somehow she found time to make beautiful embroidery work or handcrafted decorations for home and church. Besides, periodically she joined with relatives and neighbors in preparations for the joyous festivities of weddings and the solemn wakes for deceased friends. Thus her daily work was never done until all of the children were tucked away for the night on pallets unrolled and spread upon the floor.

In the midst of all of this, that couple had a great zest for life. They prayed and sang, danced and laughed, quarreled and made up, loved and begat more children.

In a general sense these two hardy pioneers have no names, but among their many descendants in each family they do have names. Word has been handed down, and stories have been told, about this ancestral pair, so that most of those of the present generation know the names of those in their lineage who fit this description. Or, if not, then certainly they should know the identity of those who deserve a place of familial eminence for having been courageous pioneers in making new homes for their progeny.

IX   Courage Without Reward

After 1840 the Texans cast covetous eyes toward New Mexico and the lucrative trade conducted over the Santa Fe Trail. By having established the southern boundary of their independent republic at the Río Grande, they claimed that that meant all of the way up that river, which would have made eastern New Mexico a part of Texas. In 1841 their ambitious president sent an expedition of more than 200 men to open trade with Santa Fe, he said; but such a large band of well armed soldiers obviously had another motive — conquest.

Fortunately for the New Mexicans the invaders had many of their horses stolen by the Indians, got lost on *El Llano Estacado*, ran short of provisions, and came straggling in scattered groups into villages along the eastern foothills. Because then they were more hungry than militant, Governor Manuel Armijo and the Mexican militia easily rounded them up and incarcerated many in the jail in San Miguel del Bado and others in neighboring villages.

The guards in San Miguel would not let their prisoners converse with any of the Americans who came traveling through that town, but some among the residents were friendly. A woman for example, who was the wife of a shoemaker, secretly brought food to the prisoners.

Another sympathetic resident was a man by the name of Gregorio Vigil. When the soldiers led forth a group of the Texans and lined them up to be executed by a firing squad, he ran in front of the captives and begged that their lives be spared. If the soldiers had fired their muskets, they would have shot down that well known citizen and erstwhile *alcalde*; therefore the captain relented and led the Texans back to jail. Vigil thus had saved the lives of those men and probably of others who might have been lined up next for execution.

Some said that this happened in San Miguel, but others thought that it happened to some of the prisoners being retained in another village farther down the river, at La Cuesta. However, since Father Stanley found that Don Gregorio owned property in El Pueblo, more than likely that was the place.

Be that as it may, certainly it was a courageous deed. However, that the Mexicans themselves did not regard Vigil as an especially important person is evidenced by the fact that when he appeared in

Las Vegas later in the same year, the *alcalde* granted him a strip of land 100 *varas* wide, or less than the average allottment, over in the valley of Agua Zarca, a small stream southwest of town. Perhaps this was because he had befriended men who apparently had been sent to conquer their province.

Although Gregorio was related to the wealthy Vigils of Santa Fe, he did not share in that wealth. Moreover, apparently he did not stay very long on that small tract near Las Vegas, because the next revelation about him is that when he died in 1853, he was an impoverished resident of Los Padillas, below Albuquerque.

Those Texans and the journalists accompanying them, whose lives had been spared, and who recorded this incident, remained grateful to Gregorio, who in their opinion was a brave man whose intervention merited for him a place of eminence in the annals of New Mexico.

This massive church building of 1806 in the formerly thriving San Miguel del Vado no doubt was the place of worship of three of the subjects of this series — Gregorio Vigil, Juan de Dios Maese, and Donaciano Vigil (Historic Preservation Bureau; photo by Federici).

X   The Doña of Tomé

In the critical year 1846 prominent New Mexicans were engaged in a Great Debate. Since this province long had been neglected by Spain and then Mexico, and since Governor Manuel Armijo was not popular in all circles, should they welcome the imposition of a new government by the United States? Or should they heed the warning of *el jefe político* about the evil treatment which *Los Americanos* would inflict upon their women and churches and repond to his plea to rally in support of the militia and to donate to him their silverware so that he would have the means to strengthen the defense?

A place where many held meetings to discuss their role was a large, plush gambling hall located on the corner of San Francisco Street and Burro Alley in Santa Fe. The proprietor, Doña Tules Barceló (Tules was a familiar abbreviation of Gertrudis), had many friends in high places, including the governor himself, because they patronized her *sala*. In addition, counted among her friends were the many Anglo traders, who also contributed much to the prosperity of her business. Perhaps it was because she was *simpático* toward them that she influenced a sentiment in opposition to her friend, the governor, who consequently was deserted by many of his erstwhile supporters among *los políticos* and *los capitanes*.

After Armijo had fled and the Army of the West had entered *La Ciudad*, Doña Tules is said to have lent General Stephen Watts Kearny $1,000 so that he could advance his soldiers partial payment prior to the arrival of their pay from the East. In addition, when Colonel Alexander Doniphan was preparing to depart on a campaign down *El Camino Real* into Chihuahua, she is reported to have advanced funds to help finance that expedition.

What is known about that influential *señora*? Contemporary observers, Josiah Gregg, Susan Shelby Magoffin, and William W.H. Davis, wrote that she had come from Taos to Santa Fe, where she had acquired great wealth as a card dealer and as a subsequent proprietor of a hall which also was a house of ill repute. Because she was a confidante of the governor, gossip added that she also was his mistress, although by 1846 she was described as a rather scrawny old woman. The legend about her origin and character continued to grow and persist. Ralph Emerson Twitchell wrote that she had a "shady reputation," Ruth Laughlin gave free play to her imagination

The influential Doña Tules was portrayed rather unattractively in this contemporary sketch published in Harper's Monthly Magazine *in 1854 (Museum of New Mexico).*

in her novel, and Father Stanley wrote that she was noted "more for her sympathy than for her virtue."

That a sensational tale dies hard is evidenced by the fact that little notice has been given to an article by Fray Angélico Chávez published in *El Palacio* in 1950. He found, first, that early writers had her arriving from the wrong direction, as she had come not from Taos of *El Río Arriba* but from Tomé of *El Río Abajo*. There Gerturdis Barceló (note the accent on the "o") was married to

Manuel Sisneros in 1823, and the couple had the social standing which accorded them entitlement as *Don* and *Doña*.

After they moved to Santa Fe, there is no question about her emergence as a "big time operator" who had much wealth and influence; but rumors about her loose conduct can be discounted, because through all of the years there she had a steadfast husband, and the slanderous comments of Anglo observers would have been influenced by provincialism. Their "Puritanical" background naturally would lead them, in those days, to imagine the worst about a woman who dealt cards and smoked cigarettes.

The aforementioned Davis, while writing sympathetically about the Mexican people, included examples of the high burial fees levied by the clergymen. For Doña Gertrudis Barceló, when she died in 1852, he wrote that the fee was close to 1,600 *pesos*; but he erred by adding that it was charged by "Biship Ortiz," whereas Lamy was the bishop and Ortiz, formerly the Vicar, was one of the executors of the Barceló estate. Further, Fray Angélico found that in the burial records the fees were noted after most other names, but after hers there was no entry.

Nevertheless, since Davis did his writing soon after the demise of Doña Tules, the assumption can be that he had the sum correct, because, to compensate for the inability of *los pobres* to pay much of a fee, if any, the clergy stuck *los ricos* for all they could get from them, and most of them did not mind that at all. The executors were willing to pay well, as the survivors relished having an ostentatious procession and mass. At any rate, the fee exacted for Doña Gertrudis Barceló does attest to the great wealth and high social standing of that influential *doña*.

XI   The Deposed Governor

This man, who originally resided on a ranch near Albuquerque, and who had a checkered career, was Manuel Armijo.

In 1827 he became sufficiently eminent that he received an appointment as governor of this Mexican province. That time in his two years in office he was credited with having strengthened the defense by reorganizing the local companies of militia.

For a time Armijo was a member of the *Diputación*, which was an advisory council for the Mexican governors in Santa Fe, and in 1836, after the chief customs officer had been ousted for misappropriating funds, he obtained that appointment. At a salary of 4,000 *pesos* a year, it was the most lucrative political plum in the province. He was irked, therefore, when a newly appointed Mexican governor, Albino Pérez, put him out.

As a result, after the Pueblo Indians of Taos had rebelled against Pérez in 1837, and had murdered him, Armijo joined with their leaders in forming a new government. Apparently disappointed by their choice of an Indian as governor instead of him, he led a counterrevolution in which the volunteers he commanded, aided by a company sent up from Mexico, defeated the Indians in a battle near Pojoaque and executed their leaders. For this he was rewarded by appointment again as governor.

Armijo's tenure was secure after he led forth the militia in 1841 and rounded up the Texans who apparently had been sent to conquer New Mexico, but who, instead, suffered from poor leadership and wandered into eastern villages. The captives then were herded together and driven on a forced march in cold weather to Mexico City; but Armijo was not responsible for their cruel treatment. For that the captain in charge was removed and court-martialed in El Paso.

Next, again Armijo strengthened the militia in several towns, levied a tax of 500 *pesos* on each wagon entering New Mexico on the Santa Fe Trail, rallied support by warning that he expected an invasion from the United States, and aroused sentiment against Anglo traders residing in Santa Fe. Moreover, it appeared that he thought he should give away most of New Mexico, before it could fall into alien hands, by making enormous grants of land to a few favored, influential residents.

When the invasion did occur in 1846, Armijo collected silverware from people and priests for the purchase of arms and ordered the militia to prepare earthworks and artillery for the making of a stand in Apache Canyon. When his officers argued that an attempt at defense would be useless, he hastily departed for Mexico; but he returned later to make his home at Lemitar.

Manuel Armijo experienced both triumphs and turmoil during his long term as the last Mexican governor (Museum of New Mexico).

In the evaluation of Armijo's career two versions emerged. He was praised, of course, by those *dons* who had received from him generous grants of land and other favors. The Mexican clergy of the province applauded him, because they had exaggerated ideas about the impending ill effects of the religious freedom which they knew that the government of the United States espoused. Especially did the conservatives in the Mexican government laud him for his efforts to strengthen the defense, his harassment of the "dangerous foreigners," and his attempt to defend New Mexico.

When he was tried in Mexico for his final failure, he was exonerated, due to his allegations that his defecting officers and soldiers were more at fault. From the point of view there, he had been a loyal patriot through it all.

On the other hand, contemporary Anglo visitors and subsequent authors propagated a less complimentary version. They repeated rumors that originally he had begun acquiring wealth by gambling and by stealing sheep, and that after Pérez had removed him from a lucrative office, he secretly had sent out agents to foment the rebellion against Pérez. They described him as a boastful man of imposing appearance, who, as he rode on his mule in Santa Fe, lashed with his whip any of *los pobres* who got in his way. In addition, he was rumored to have had several mistresses, including perhaps a wealthy woman, "Doña Tules," owner of a gambling house.

When Armijo led the counter revolution, he was said to have bribed his officers to send favorable reports about him to Mexico, and when the occupying army was approaching, allegedly he accepted a bribe from an advance emissary, who persuaded him to pretend to make a stand but to withdraw at the last minute. Then, after he had fled to Mexico, there were suspicions that he had carted away with him much of the silverware he had collected.

Those who capitalized upon those derogatory rumors in later years could do so freely, without fear of causing affront to many others by the name of Armijo, because that deposed governor had only an adopted daughter and therefore no direct descendants.

Whichever version may be accepted as plausible, certainly Armijo had been a man of great eminence in the eventful early history of New Mexico.

XII   Center of the Storm

Two miles west of Taos a large adobe house, built shortly after 1800, now is on the National Register of Historic Places. It has been honored because it is a well preserved example of an early headquarters of a *hacienda*, which was long occupied by Don Severino Martínez and his family. It happened, too, that one of his sons, Antonio José, was destined to become a famous priest of the mid-nineteenth century.

In 1798 Antonio's wealthy father sent the bright lad, at the age of five, to a good school in Abiquiú, where the family then resided. There the boy excelled in his studies, which included learning English.

In 1812 he married a girl selected by his parents, as was the custom then, but a year later Antonio was greatly saddened when she died during childbirth. Then it was that he resolved to become a priest. Later, in 1825, he also lost his beloved daughter.

Long afterward his critics spread a slander about his harboring a harem and having many illegitimate offspring; but a scholar who has researched the matter thoroughly, Ray John de Aragón, has concluded that that had to have arisen by mistaking him for one of several others by the name of Antonio Martínez. Besides, in a home which the *padre* later maintained for orphans of parents killed in warfare, the children often called him their "father," which could have contributed to a false impression.

After intensive research, Fray Angélico Chávez also concluded that later claimants of this famous man as an ancestor must have been only of "collateral descent." On the other hand, he found that this *padre* had secret "trysts" with a Manuela Romero from 1831 to 1837 and that some mysteries did evolve from that "concubinage."

Anyhow, from 1817 to 1823 Antonio progressed well with his studies in the seminary in Durango, and during that time, in 1821, Mexico became independent of Spain. In 1825 he received an assignment as assistant to the priest in Tomé, and a year later he was placed in charge of the Parish of Abiquiú and also given an appointment as curator in the Parish of Taos, to which was added the Mission of Picurís in 1829.

He began writing articles about the hardships imposed upon his people by the tithes strictly exacted of them by the clergy, and he also became a superior in the Order of Penitentes. Although both

The headquarters of the Severino Martínez Ranch near Taos, built short-ly after 1800, was then the home of the youthful Antonio José Martínez, who became a famous priest (Historic Preservation Bureau; photo by Federici).

of those activities were frowned upon by the higher clergy, Aragón found reports in which the Bishop of Durango nevertheless continued to commend him for diligent fulfillment of his wide range of duties.

In 1833 in Taos the *padre* opened a seminary, which trained several young men for the priesthood. Two years later he obtained a printing press, by which he produced school books he had written. He then began publishing a newspaper, *El Crepúsculo*, in which he protested against the new direct taxes imposed by the Mexican governor, Albino Pérez, who was appointed in 1835. Thus Padre Martínez could be suspected of instigating the rebellion of the Taos Indians in 1837, yet he was reported to have tried to dissuade them from resorting to violence.

His pleas went unheeded. The angry Indians overwhelmed the governor's feeble forces, murdered him, and established their own government in Santa Fe. During the brief tenure of the Indians there, this *padre* joined them and helped draft for them their statement of grievances against Mexico.

After the Army of the West had occupied New Mexico in 1846, Padre Martínez expressed interest in the democratic principles of the new government, sought to render helpful services to it, and again tried to restrain opponents from resorting to violence, but to no avail. Those in Taos rebelled in January, 1847, and murdered most of the Anglos there, for which American soldiers furiously assaulted the Taos Pueblo.

When Jean Baptiste Lamy, a Frenchman, came from Kentucky in 1851 to serve first as vicar apostolic and later as bishop and archbishop, he untactfully criticized the "immorality" of the resident Spanish Americans, and then he, too, imposed severe collection of tithes and high burial fees. As the bishop encountered opposition by native priests, and expelled two of them, Padre Martínez protested in their defense. That and his continued writings in behalf of the poor people of his jurisdiction finally resulted in excommunication of him by Bishop Lamy in 1857. Then, in the words of Fray Angélico, his relations with Lamy changed from friendly "pathetic pleading to bitter invective."

The deposed *padre* and many of his parishioners refused to recognize the priest whom Lamy sent to replace him. As he continued to fight the bishop's edict, as "illegal," the struggle took its toll on him. He became ill and died in 1867. Thus the Hispanos of northern New Mexico lost prematurely the advocacy in their behalf by this persistent champion of justice and democracy.

XIII   The First Governor

The name of the first effective governor of New Mexico under American administration, Donaciano Vigil, does not appear in some of the published lists of governors, although he is named in the list printed in the *New Mexico Blue Book*. Usually a roll call of Mexican governors ends with the name of Manuel Armijo, and a list of United States territorial governors usually begins with James S. Calhoun, the first congressional appointee. Moreover, Miguel A. Otero, Jr., is often credited with having been the first Hispanic governor, but Vigil had that distinction.

How did this come about? It fell upon Donaciano to serve as governor in a transitional period from 1847 to 1848, which was the most difficult era in the history of New Mexico. When General Stephen Watts Kearny had appointed Charles Bent as interim governor, he also had named Vigil as his secretary, or the equivalent of lieutenant governor. After Bent was killed in the Pueblo Rebellion in Taos in January, 1847, Vigil had to assume the gubernatorial duties, which he fulfilled well until a military commander relieved him in 1848.

Father Stanley traced Donaciano's lineage back to distinguished soldiers in Spain, one of whom, Francisco Montes de Vigil came, with his wife, to New Spain, and research by Fray Angélico reveals that his family was among the pioneers of the seventeenth century in New Mexico.

In Santa Fe, Don Francisco prospered so well that the Vigils became one of the wealthy families in *La Ciudad*. Moreover, the military tradition prevailed, as nearly all of the Vigils were soldiers. Francisco's grandson, who was Donaciano's father, deviated from the military stereotype, because he also was a "bookworm," who gathered up and read all of the books he could find. Further, besides sending his children to school, he gave them much instruction at home.

The outcome was that later Donaciano became recognized as one of the best educated, and most scholarly, men in Santa Fe. Meanwhile, Donaciano was participating in frequent campaigns against Navajos and Apaches while posted in Santa Fe and briefly in San Miguel del Bado. As could be expected, constantly he urged his fellow soldiers also to become literate and learned.

It happened that Vigil's superior officer, an arrogant man who apparently was jealous of this sergeant, deliberately provoked him into minor acts of insubordination, for which Donaciano was sent to jail. Thus this future governor spent some time in the lockup in Santa Fe, just as Otero did, subsequently.

During the Pueblo Rebellion of 1837, said to have been fomented secretly by Manuel Armijo and his cohorts, Vigil escaped from jail, organized a company to fight in behalf of the Mexican governor, Albino Pérez, and failed in that effort. Pérez was ousted and beheaded.

Nevertheless, the new governor, Armijo, soon took notice of this tall (6'5"), scholarly soldier and employed him as his secretary. In ensuing years, while Donaciano was hobnobbing with American traders in order to learn all he could from them, he was also loyally traveling around in an effort to arouse the Mexican citizens to prepare for defense against an anticipated invasion by the United States. In addition, in 1844 he founded a newspaper in Santa Fe, *La Verdad*, which was the second in the territory, after *El Crepúsculo*, published by Padre Martínez in Taos.

When the expected invasion occurred, and the Mexican army was disbanded, the former Captain Vigil was merely a spectator when his cousin was selected for the obligatory responsibility of heading a committee which welcomed the inauguration of American occupation and pledged the people's loyalty to the new government.

Vigil's retirement was short-lived, because the attention of General Kearny soon was attracted to him, and then Kearny employed him, along with two eastern lawyers, to draft a new code of laws. Vigil's contribution was that he influenced the embodiment in the Kearny Code of provisions peculiar to New Mexico and favorable to its Hispanic people.

Next came his aforementioned appointment as secretary to Bent, which he accepted reluctantly, followed by his term as governor. Then he assembled a convention to try to obtain immediate statehood for New Mexico, without success. His testimony in behalf of many citizens helped them retain possession of their land, and his investigations prepared the way for later retention of Spanish land grants by the several Indian Pueblos. He drafted rules for instituting a system of circuit courts, along with a criminal code for the guidance of the sheriffs. He supervised the prefects in the counties in reorganizing the militia. He had a committee select a site

Donaciano Vigil house in Santa Fe
(Historic Preservation Bureau; photo by Federici).

for a university near Santa Fe and appointed a board for it, but afterward *políticos* frustrated that ambition. Meanwhile he was donating all of his salary for assistance to impoverished families.

Afterward, for the new government he headed the Board of Supervisors of Education and served terms periodically in the territorial legislature. He also led in founding a village near the abandoned Pecos Pueblo, and in 1855 he moved there, where he acquired much land in that vicinity. When he died in 1877, his funeral, according to Ralph Emerson Twitchell, attracted the greatest crowd ever assembled in Santa Fe for that kind of a tribute to a deceased citizen.

Why has this eminent Hispano been accorded meagre recognition by historians? One reason is that in that critical era he was caught in a peculiar position. As a former loyal officer in the army of an enemy, he avoided attracting attention to himself while allowing Anglo newcomers to get most of the credit for his contributions behind the scenes. In addition, as one who had transferred his loyalty, and services, so promptly and fully to the new government, he sought to do that unostentatiously in order to avoid criticism by, and to solicit the cooperation of, other citizens also formerly loyal to Mexico. Most influential, however, was the fact that by all accounts he was a self-effacing man, who did not seek office and the recognition which it might bring. Public service to his people was his paramount concern, and that was a commendable personal ideal.

XIV   From Priesthood to Politics

New Mexico has acquired a reputation for having its own "peculiar brand" of politics. Winning election to an office in order to have dispensation of its patronage became a prevalent social objective. As a result, many campaigns have been heated contests for which often the ballot boxes were impounded, and sometimes the National Guard was called out to keep order.

For example, there was that clash in Mesilla in 1871, as described by William A. Keleher. During the campaign for election of a delegate to Congress, which in territorial days was the highest office filled by the voters, local Democrats planned a rally in support of José Manuel Gallegos, and the Republicans scheduled one for the same hour in behalf of J. Francisco Chávez. As both crowds paraded around the plaza in opposite directions, a head-on collision became an outright battle which left nine men dead and 40 to 50 injured.

Since Chávez is the subject of another profile in this series, his opponent, Gallegos, is the subject of this one. First, back in the Mexican Period, he had been one of the priests who had received his training in the seminary conducted in Taos by Padre Martínez, and then he had been assigned to a populous parish in Albuquerque. There he had become so influential and popular that in 1843 he had been appointed as a member of the Departmental *Asamblea*, which was the council of advisers to the governor in the Mexican regime.

After the occupation of New Mexico by the Army of the West in the autumn of 1846, Padre José Manuel Gallegos was at first rebellious. He is alleged to have been one of the men who slyly fomented the uprising in Taos against United States administration in January, 1847, which was forcibly subdued. Next, his opposition was aroused when Jean Baptiste Lamy, a Frenchman, arrived from Kentucky in 1851 as vicar apostolic and began asserting control over the native priests.

The local clergy, who previously had been under the jurisdiction of the Bishop of Durango, suspected that Lamy was an imposter, until the latter made a trip to Durango in order to get a statement from the bishop affirming that north of the border Lamy truly was in charge. Even then some of the more outspoken clergymen, including Padre Gallegos, resisted innovations made by Lamy.

In 1852, while Lamy was in the East, Padre Gallegos obtained the

45

consent of Lamy's assistant, the Rev. Joseph P. Machebeuf, to make a trip to Durango. Under the circumstances the purpose of that journey could be questioned; therefore when Lamy returned, he suspended Gallegos for having made an "unlawful trip." Then hundreds of his parishioners sent Lamy a petition requesting the reinstatement of their popular *padre*, but Lamy refused to yield. He sent Father Machebeuf to Albuquerque to replace Padre Gallegos.

This incident has been cited by critics of Lamy as an example of his unjustifiably arbitrary performance, and certainly he was arbitrary when he said, as quoted by Ray John de Aragón, "it is my business alone." On the other hand, the Rev. William J. Howlett, writing in 1908, found evidence in the Machebeuf papers that Padre Gallegos "drank, gambled, and danced" in the company of several of his wealthy parishioners. Since Lamy had been openly critical of the conduct of Spanish Americans, he would not tolerate that kind of behavior by a priest. Machebeuf had recorded that as the real reason, and in his opinion a justifiable one, for the prompt dismissal of Gallegos as a priest.

Then José Manuel Gallegos decided to go into politics as a citizen converted to loyalty to the United States. In 1853 he won election as New Mexico's delegate to Congress, but when he sought reelection in 1855, the campaign between him and Miguel A. Otero, Sr., of Valencia County resurrected issues in his dispute with Bishop Lamy. After a hotly contested debate of pros and cons about Lamy, Gallegos lost on that platform that time.

In 1857 Gallegos moved to Santa Fe and built a house which is still preserved as a historic property. He ran for election to the legislature, won, and subsequently won reelection thrice. His good record led to his election as Speaker of the House. In 1871 he again sought to go to Washington as New Mexico's delegate, and that is when the aforementioned "battle" occurred in La Mesilla. In that contest he defeated one of the more popular and influential of the Republican leaders, J. Francisco Chávez. In his long career he also held an appointment in the 1860s as Superintendent of Indian Affairs, and later he served a term as Territorial Treasurer.

Certainly arousing the ire of the bishop by Padre Gallegos had resulted in a personal decision by which New Mexico had gained a spirited, respected holder of public offices for many years thereafter.

XV   One Man Army

Along the west central border of New Mexico lies one of the younger counties of the state, created in 1921 and named after Thomas Benton Catron. Since that is rugged country, it is sparsely populated, now having an average of only three persons for each square mile. In earlier times it was the western portion of a very large Socorro County, and "Frisco" was the nickname of the town which preceded Reserve, the present county seat.

In the early 1880s Texas cowboys often went on a rampage in Frisco, and especially did that happen when the Slaughter outfit went through on a cattle drive. One day in 1884, as one by the name of McCarthy, on a drunken spree, was riding up and down the street and shooting wildly, a nineteen-year-old deputy sheriff, Élfego Baca, happened to ride in from Socorro. He urged the justice of the peace to arrest that man, who was endangering people's lives; but the justice refused, because he feared retribution by the Slaughter gang.

Élfego arrested the offender, and, according to one version, the justice, in a crowded court room, rendered a verdict of "guilty" and set the fine at only five dollars, whereupon Baca withdrew in disgust to a cabin in the Mexican part of town. There a mob of 80 Texans swooped down upon him for allegedly having shot a man in the tussle while he was making the arrest. Of the four who came near, Baca shot one in the stomach.

By the other version, because the justice was too scared to hear the case, Élfego took McCarthy with him to the Mexican section, and there Slaughter's crowd followed him and demanded that he release the rowdy. Then Baca opened fire, wounded one man, and shot the horse of another, which fell on its rider and killed him.

Either way, Baca finally fled to a remote *jacal*, whose occupant was absent, and holed up in it. Since the walls of a *jacal* were built by driving posts in the ground and plastering the cracks with mud, it did not afford much protection, as the 80 assaulting Texans fired volley after volley into it, some said from an arroyo and others said from behind an adobe wall. Baca occasionally sniped at them, killing four.

When the bullet-ridden stakes gave way at one corner, part of the hut caved in upon Élfego; but he just lay there for two hours, benefitting from that added protection, before he removed the debris. Near midnight the besiegers, according to some observers, blew up one end of the shack with a stick of dynamite, but Élfego was in the other end of the building. As others related it, that night the cowboys threw firebrands on the hut, which failed to ignite, because it had a dirt roof. Perhaps the baffled Texans tried both of those tactics.

After a siege of 33 hours a deputy sheriff brought to the scene a Spanish-American friend of Baca and had him promise a safe escort to Socorro if he would surrender. He came out then, and for assurance of his safety, he refused to hand over his pistols. In the ensuing trial in Albuquerue a jury of his peers acquitted him of the charges of murder, because he had fired in self defense.

J.H. Cook, a participant who wrote a description of this battle, missed an important detail, which was filled in by interviews made in 1938 by W.P.A. writers with others who had heard first-hand accounts. They learned that the *jacal* had a dirt floor excavated about one foot below ground level. What Baca did was to lie down on that floor, and the bullets whizzed through above him. It was estimated that altogether 4,000 shots were fired into that hut, and by actual count there were 367 bullet holes in the door. The cowboys therefore came to regard Baca's miraculous survival as evidence that he had a charmed existence.

As the legend about Élfego's invincibility spread throughout the county, several times it stood him in good stead. In rough and tumble clashes in behalf of friends, as described by his biographer, Kyle Crichton, and later in some impending crises while he was sheriff of Socorro County in 1919 to 1920, all he had to do to wilt the opposition was to announce that, "I am Élfego Baca."

Meanwhile he had acquired an education and had been admitted to the bar. His popularity and ability had won him election as county clerk, mayor, school superintendent, and district attorney, all between 1893 and 1906. Next had come an exciting interlude in El Paso and Juárez during the revolution in Mexico, as related by Crichton and also by Byron A. Johnson writing in *La Crónica*. To sum it up briefly, he became entangled in the rivalry between Mexican leaders, with the result that once Pancho Villa offered a reward of $30,000 for his capture; but he evaded that threat. He was also employed as the foreman of fourteen guards, or "bouncers," in the Tivoli gambling hall in Juárez at a salary of $750 a month.

After his term as sheriff back in Socorro, he and his law partner opened an office in Albuquerque. Even then in his legal practice occasionally he resorted to irregular tactics which sometimes, as before, stood him "on both sides of the law," in the words of Johnson. Finally, in 1945 he passed away quietly after a lifetime of adventures, including especially that thrilling youthful "battle" in which he, as a "one man army," had held at bay 80 irate, frustrated cowboys.

Elfego Baca, Socorro, New Mexico, 1880's.

XVI   Patrones Rurales

The first "long drives" were not of cattle from Texas to railheads in Kansas, but rather of sheep from New Mexico down *El Camino Real* to cities in Mexico. The earliest of great magnitude was made by Francisco Chávez, the leading sheep rancher of the Mexican Period, who is said to have driven 75,000 into Mexico in 1839. After the discovery of gold in California, drives were made to the mining towns, notably by another Chávez, J. Francisco, who took 25,000 there in 1853, and by Antonio José Luna and Antonio José Otero, who together drove 50,000 there in the early 1850s (Yes, the two men had the same given names).

Those long drives were risky ordeals, sometimes ending in disaster; but if successful, the price of $10 to $15 a head commanded in the market in California made the rancher the equivalent of a modern millionaire. For others the marketing of the wool, alone, was profitable. As a result, in 1850 almost 400,000 sheep were being grazed in New Mexico, and by 1880 the number was approaching three million.

The large land grants made in early times were for the purpose of ranching, but in some instances they were disposed of for development by others, not Hispanic. Examples are the mammoth grant made to Pablo Montoya, which became the nucleus of the Bell Ranch, and another made to Guadalupe Miranda and Charles Beaubien, jointly, which became the Maxwell Ranch.

Because the grazing land was in large tracts, nearly all owned by *dons*, small operators usually had to enter into a *partidario*, or sharecropping, agreement with a *don*, and the latter thus engaged many men to carry the responsibility of grazing his sheep. Typically, the *pastor* borrowed a number of head and agreed to a specified fee for use of the grazing land. He could keep a certain proportion of the lambs, but he was obligated to deliver to the *patrón* nearly all of the wool gleaned from the original ewes and to return the original number of them at the end of, say, five years. Because the *pastores* assumed all of the costs and risks, often they became inextricably indebted to the *patrón*. Under that prevalent *partido* system many of *los ricos* grew *mas ricos*.

Even where villagers had access to the common pastures of the large community land grants, many of them could obtain sheep only under *partidos* granted by the owners of thousands — either some

50

of the wealty *dons* or the thriving commission houses of that era. Exceptions occurred there and on some of the large ranches, in that several *patrones* preferred to employ many *pastores* at the current low wages instead of engaging them as *partidarios*.

One of the big ranchers, J. Francisco Chávez of Valencia County, is the subject of another sketch in this series. Antonio José Luna, also a leading rancher in that county, was the father of Solomón Luna, who also is given separate attention.

Farther south, near Socorro, Leandro Baca was the owner of a large ranch at Lajoya, and he did his marketing of wool by operating a caravan of wagons on overland freighting trips. For several years he also held county offices.

To the north, near Taos, Juan Santistevan grazed 35,000 sheep on a large ranch, and he, too, shipped his wool to market. For fourteen years he was the postmaster in Taos.

Also near Taos, a prosperous rancher was Severino Martínez who has been mentioned previously as the father of Padre Antonio José Martínez.

An earlier rancher near Taos was Diego Romero, who obtained his land grant in 1724 and erected a complex of buildings facing a large yard, which later became the Plaza of Ranchos de Taos.

Around Galisteo, south of Santa Fe, José Ortiz, known as *El Patrón*, in the era around 1900 grazed about 60,000 sheep under the supervision of his employed *mayordomos* and *caporales*, to whom the *pastores* and *camperos* were responsible for the care of the flocks while encamped at many propitious locations.

In Upper Las Vegas, José Albino Baca was able to build a three story mansion in the 1850s as a result of wealth acquired from the grazing of thousands of sheep in that vicinity under the traditional *partido* system.

A greater variety of production was possible in sheltered locations near an ample source of water for irrigation and near a market for produce. Then fruit orchards and crops of grain could be cultivated.

El Rancho Viejo near Santa Fe, developed in the 1840s by a wealthy politician, Juan Bautista Vigil y Alarid, became noted for its great orchard of productive fruit trees.

At La Cueva, near Mora, Vicente Romero bought up parcels of land until he had amassed 33,000 acres. By developing one of the best irrigation systems in the territory he, too, cultivated a large fruit orchard and also produced much grain for sale to the Army,

51

This mansion, built in the 1850's at La Cueva, near Mora, was the headquarters of a large, productive ranch, owned then by Vicente Romero (Historic Preservation Bureau; photo by Federici).

especially at Fort Union.

Cattle ranching on the grasslands was a later development, largely by Anglo newcomers. However, there were also Spanish-American cattlemen. One was Celso Baca, who acquired a large ranch at present Santa Rosa. Since he raised both cattle and sheep, he marketed wool by putting a caravan of wagons on the Santa Fe Trail. He is remembered for having built a chapel dedicated to the first saint in the New World, Santa Rosa de Lima, from which the city there derived its name.

For a special reason another ranch must be mentioned. It, Las Golondrinas at La Ciénega, near Santa Fe, dates back to 1650. Developed by Vega and Baca families in succession, it became a convenient stopping place for travelers on *El Camino Real*. Beginning in 1932, and especially since 1971, it has become a popular, educational tourist attraction by the maintenance there of a large museum and the creation of a typical mountain village by transplanting there a *morada*, a winery, a grist mill, and other buildings to supplement the charming old ranch house.

This summary is by no means comprehensive. It presents only a sampling of the emergence of prosperous and influential Hispanic ranchers in various locations in New Mexico prior to statehood.

XVII The Eminent Boss

While J. Francisco Chávez was emerging in the esteem of contemporary writers as "the foremost citizen of New Mexico," he also was incurring the political oppostion of two other foremost families in Valencia County, the Lunas and the Oteros. All three, having distinguished lineages, also had become wealthy ranchers, and the Lunas and Oteros will put in their appearance later in these pages.

The conflict became so bitter that the priest who had all three families as parishioners once wrote in his diary that he was growing weary of hearing their confessions. Then the territorial legislature intervened. In 1903 that body cut off the part of the county east of the mountains and as Gilberto Espinosa related, handed it over to Don J. Francsco, who then moved east to Pino Wells. The legislature named it "Torrance County," because back in 1889 another county already had been named "Chaves" in recognition of this foremost citizen.

The Chávez, or Chaves, lineage can be traced back to Pedro Durán y Chávez who had come in 1600 to join the colony founded by Juan de Oñate at San Juan. J. Francisco, who was born in 1833, had as his father Mariano Chaves and as his grandfather Francisco Xavier Chávez, both of whom had served terms as governor. Like several other sons of *dons*, this lad went to St. Louis University and thence to New York, where he studied medicine.

Upon his return he found the territory in the midst of the turmoil created by the Civil War. He enlisted in the Union Army, was commissioned as captain, served under Colonel Kit Carson in the campaign to round up the Navajos, fought against the Confederates in the Battle of Valverde early in 1862, and later in that year, advanced to a lieutenant-colonelcy, he supervised the moving of Fort Wingate to its permanent location.

After the war had ended, he ran on the Republican ticket for election as New Mexico's delegate in Congress, won then, and won reelection twice. Only three others had the distinction of serving three terms as delegate, and among them was one of those Oteros, Miguel A., Sr. While Colonel Chávez was in Washington, the Congress enacted a law in 1868 abolishing peonage in New Mexico. It liberated the hundreds of Indian captives held as servants by the numerous *dons*. J. Francisco, himself the owner of several Indian servants, vigorously opposed it as violating a long-standing

This engraving shows the Plaza of Albuquerque as it appeared in the 1850's, when José Manuel Gallegos was a popular local priest (Museum of New Mexico, from W.W.H. Davis, El Gringo).

"tradition" of the territory; but that local tradition then had to give way to a national tradition emerging from the war — the liberation of slaves.

Upon his return to New Mexico, he studied law, gained admission to the bar, and won election to the territorial House of Representatives in 1875. Thenceforth he was reelected regularly to the House and later to the Council, which then was the equivalent of a Senate. Because in his service there he demonstrated a keen interest in the school system, in 1901 he was appointed Superintendent of Public Instruction and reappointed in 1903. One of his biographers, Paul A. F. Walter, wrote that he "did more to develop the schools than anyone, especially in rural districts." While he was absorbed in the promotion of practical methods of instruction for Spanish-American pupils in poorer, rural areas, the legislature also appointed him as Territorial Historian in 1903, whereupon he became absorbed in the task of collecting historical information.

In the year 1903 he moved to Pinos Wells in the new county in which he was the "boss." There one evening in November, 1904, a man stole into his house and shot him while he was dining with some friends. Because he had been firm and fearless in his opposition to the tactics of some of the *politicos* in Santa Fe, rumor had it that "higher ups" had hired a "hit-man" to assassinate him. On the other hand, he had also gathered evidence against men who were involved in rustling and vandalism in his new county, and that aroused a suspicion that one of them had done away with him. At any rate, nobody was ever convicted for the perpetrating of this mysterious murder of one of the most eminent, veteran legislators of that era.

XVIII   The Sage and the Soldier

Since the Spanish word for "moon" is feminine, it would seem that the name of the city should be *Las Lunas*; but, as well informed Hispanos are aware, the city was named after the Luna families residing there, and thus it is "Los Lunas." There are other family place names in New Mexico, for example, Los Vigiles, Los Padillas, Los Montoyas, and Los Chávez.

When Antonio José Luna, who was born in Los Lentes in 1808, needed more land for his ranching, he founded Los Lunas and promoted its development. As he grew wealthy, he bought the San Clemente Land Grant on which the settlement was located.

His son, Solomón, born in Los Lunas in 1858, had private tutors and then attended St. Louis University. He had inherited a great sheep ranch, which, according to Gilberto Espinosa, he developed into the largest in the territory in number of sheep and in capital investment.

As in the case of other *dons*, public offices beckoned him. He was elected as the probate clerk of Valencia County and later as sheriff and treasurer, but there he drew the line. Regularly he declined offers of nomination for territorial offices, although he had become so highly respected that others said he could easily have won election as the first governor or as one of the first senators of New Mexico when it became a state.

Nevertheless, he did become a member of the Republican National Committee in 1896, and he did accept election as a delegate to the convention which drafted the state constitution in 1910. In the latter proceedings he was credited with having been such an influential counselor that, according to Thomas J. Mabry, "he needed only to lift a finger or raise his eyebrows, to stop any proposal which he deemed against the best interest of his people, his party, or the proposed new state." However, he failed to get the delegates to write into the document a liberal provision which he favored — the franchise for women in school elections.

When he declined the offer of others to place his name in nomination for governor at the Republican convention in 1911, he backed Holm O. Bursum, who was nominated but failed to win the election. Soon afterward, in 1912, Solomón Luna died suddenly of a stroke at the age of 54. That terminated prematurely his promising career as an influential counselor in state affairs.

Solomón Luna, wealthy rancher of Luna County, had an influential role in politics and in the drafting of the State Constitution in 1910 (Museum of New Mexico).

Solomón's nephew, Maximiliano, who was born in Los Lunas in 1870, obtained his education in the college which was maintained by Jesuits in Las Vegas from 1877 to 1888 and in Georgetown University near Washington, D.C. Upon his return he, too, entered politics by filling successfully county offices for four years, and then, when he was only 26 years old, he won election to the territorial House of Representatives, where the members chose him to serve as Speaker.

When the United States went to war with Spain in April, 1898, in order to gain independence for Cuba, a regiment raised mostly in the Southwest and commanded at first by Colonel Leonard Wood and later by Colonel Theodore Roosevelt became known as the "Rough Riders." Maximiliano enlisted in it, was commissioned as captain of Troop F, and was reported to have served gallantly in the battles of Las Guasimas and San Juan Hill.

After he returned, he again became Speaker of the House. When the Normal University in Las Vegas was dedicated in March of 1899, the *Las Vegas Daily Optic* published in full the address of its president, Dr. Edgar L. Hewett, whereas the local Spanish-language newspaper singled out for high praise the remarks made by Maximiliano Luna, "because of his great work in behalf of education," the reporter said.

Soon afterward a band of Filipinos rebelled against the acquisition of their islands by the United States, and this former Rough Rider promptly reenlisted to serve again under his former commander, General Leonard Wood, in the campaign to suppress that insurrection. Unfortunately he was drowned while a detachment was crossing a flooded river in the Philippines. Never would he return again to pursue what certainly would have been a distinguished career in his home state.

Years later, after World War I, the New Mexico National Guard held its annual encampments on a *mesa* near Las Vegas. That camp was named after incumbent governors until 1929, when Colonel Norman L. King, commander of the regiment of cavalry, named it after a cavalry officer, Maximiliano Luna, who had sacrificed his life in service to his country. Since 1970 on the site of that former Camp Luna the name of the Luna Vocational-Technical Institute has perpetuated the memorial.

XIX Patrones Comerciales

Books about the Santa Fe trade portray it as a project of Midwesterners driving wagons in caravans from Missouri to New Mexico and back again. It was initiated in that manner, but very soon to a remarkable extent it became also a project of Spanish-American entrepreneurs in New Mexico.

In town after town those who could muster the means to acquire wagons and livestock put them on the Trail, and their profits usually enabled them to obtain more equipment, until some became big operators. As they hired many drivers, that brought many other men into the business.

South of Ratón Pass the main trail had a branch which crossed westward to Taos. As the main trail coursed on southward, it was joined at Watrous by the Cimarrón Cutoff, which traversed a barren country in order to avoid crossing Ratón Pass. Thence the caravans went by way of Las Vegas to Santa Fe, and from the latter place some went on southward through the towns along *El Camino Real* to Chihuahua in Mexico. Principally along those routes of travel the opportunity arose for mercantile businesses.

The wagons brought into New Mexico tools, cloth, clothing, and household conveniences — all products of the Industrial Revolution in the East. They returned loaded with wool, hides, and some handcrafted products, or else towed along many mules for sale in Missouri. After the Santa Fe Railroad built into New Mexico along that same route between 1879 and 1883, it handled that traffic along the way. In addition, it was able to transport heavier wares, as mining machinery, farm implements, and furniture.

Some merchants engaged only in the trade by wagons in the earlier years, others opened stores later for the marketing of products brought in by rail, and a few spanned both eras. Because they marked up the prices of the imported goods, for example, to $2.00 a yard for calico in the early years, several who had no big losses along the way made great profits.

Were the merchants exploiting ruthlessly the market on this frontier? In the pricing of goods, perhaps yes, although an allowance has to be made for the risks they were incurring. On the other hand, when the customers were eager buyers, they did not regard themselves as being exploited. To get a yard of cloth previously, the wool had to be sheared, washed, carded, and spun into thread,

This thriving mercantile house was established immediately after the arrival of the railroad in Las Vegas in 1879 and was moved into a new, large, brick building in 1898 (Museum of New Mexico).

Severo A. Baca, wealthy merchant and public official, constructed this building in Socorro in 1889 to house his store and place of residence (Historic Preservation Bureau; photo by Federici).

which then had to be dyed and woven — a process requiring weeks of work all by hand. So it was, too, with the fabricating of tools and furnishings in that era of domestic crafts. Consequently the customers were eager to obtain the new wares even at high prices. Although many of them had little money, they still could barter for the goods with their wool, cowhides, furs, mules, and produce.

Among the middlemen who handled the transactions the names of several Hispanos appear in the accounts. They included the Romero brothers and F.A. Manzanares in Las Vegas, Antonio Armijo and Felipe Delgado in Santa Fe, Benito Baca in Tucumcari, Felipe Chávez in Belén, Juan Nepomuceno García and Severo Baca in Socorro, and Martín Amador and Nestor Armijo in Las Cruces. No doubt there were others who now have escaped notice.

The wealthy merchants built fine homes, some of which are preserved today as cultural properties. Needless to say, they became men of considerable influence in their respective communities, and some consequently filled public offices. The highest attainments of that kind were made by Trinidad Romero and F.A. Manzanares, both of Las Vegas, who were delegates to Congress in 1877 to 1879 and 1883 to 1885, respectively.

When summed up, the emergence of these merchants represented a facet of the adaptability of the Hispanos to new conditions and the consequent rise to wealth and eminence by some of them as they capitalized upon their opportunities.

Martín Amador, proprietor of a successful freighting and express business, had this building constructed in Las Cruces in the 1880's for use originally as a hotel (Historic Preservation Bureau; photo by Federici).

61

XX   The First Superintendent

The man who was appointed as the first territorial Superintendent of Public Instruction in 1892, Amado Chaves, had had no experience as either a teacher or as an administrator. Possibly it helped that he came from a "good family," as that was a strong qualification for office in those days.

This Chaves was descended from Fernando Durán y Chaves, who had come to Santa Fe when it was reoccupied by Diego de Vargas in 1693, and then had become one of the *alcaldes* of that *villa*. Moreover, Amado was a son of Manuel Antonio Chaves, who by virtue of a record as a great campaigner against Indians had been advanced to the rank of lieutenant colonel in the New Mexico Volunteers.

In April, 1862, when invading Confederates from their camp at Cañoncito were engaged in the Battle of Glorieta against the Colorado Volunteers, it was Colonel Chaves who had guided a detachment of the latter under Major John Chivington up over Glorieta Mesa in order to swoop down upon the Confederate camp and destroy all of their wagons, mules, and supplies. Chivington took all of the credit for that victory, which caused the Texas Confederates to depart hastily from New Mexico.

Amado, who was graduated from St. Michael's College in Santa Fe, next studied law at Georgetown University. After his return to New Mexico in 1882, he developed a law practice in which he became highly regarded as a specialist on land grant problems. Then when he won election to the House of Representatives, the members chose him as its Speaker. That was the background which he had for tackling the formidable task of developing a system of schools when he obtained the appointment as superintendent.

In the early 1890s a movement was under way for improvements in public education, which had been neglected due to opposition by the clergy and the *dons*. Then other forces became influential. For one, during the long, frustrating series of efforts to gain statehood, one of the obstacles had been objections by opponents in the East, who contended that the New Mexicans had not been adequately "Americanized," due to the inadequacy of the public school system. A report prepared in 1880 revealed that the average school attendance was only a little over 3,000 out of a population of 110,000.

A statute enacted in 1884 provided for the appointment of county

As at the above school near Carlsbad in 1904, women emerged in an active role in the territorial system organized by Amado Chaves and J. Francisco Chávez (Museum of New Mexico).

superintendents, but that was not enough, as there was still no territorial system. Then at a meeting in Santa Fe in 1885 the New Mexico Education Associaton was launched. After the teachers held their first annual convention in Las Vegas during the Christmas holidays in 1887, they began lobbying effectively for improvements. They were joined in their efforts by several Populists who were elected to the legislature in 1890 during the upsurge of the People's party. Since their program for the benefit of the common man included improvements in education, those Populists were influential in getting a stronger school statute adopted in 1891 and another in 1893 providing for the founding of normal schools in Silver City and in Las Vegas.

Thus it came about that Amado Chaves swung into action in 1892 as the first superintendent. He faced a challenging task, as the new school law required that he develop a standardized selection of textbooks and an improved course of study and that he visit each county once annually to help the locally elected county superintendents conduct institutes, or training sessions, for their teachers.

This was not the kind of an appointment by which a man could engage in financial aggrandizement, as was the case with some other "political plums." That Chaves did not profit financially, and perhaps failed to break even, is evidenced by the fact that in 1902 businessmen in Santa Fe brought suit against him for his indebtedness to them amounting to $13,900. Rather, they brought suit, and attached a lien, against his share in the Las Trampas Land Grant.

Although he did not grow wealthy from his professional services, he did get credit for doing the job well. Historians, therefore, have attributed to his endeavors, and those of a successor, J. Francisco Chávez, the laying of a sound foundation for the subsequent development of a good statewide system. In their zeal to attain statehood the New Mexicans, Hispanos included, overemphasized the "Americanization" of pupils; yet certainly their demonstration of strong efforts for improvement in education, along with progress in settling titles land and in suppressing outlawry, contributed to the change of attitude in the East that facilitated the final achievement of statehood in 1912.

XXI   The Popular Governor

In his old age Miguel A. Otero, Jr., fortunately wrote his reminiscences in two books which not only are lively with interesting anecdotes but also are valuable sources for historians in their study of the territorial period in New Mexico. Otero's eventful career gave him much to write about.

In the first place, his father had set for him an illustrious example. Born in Valencia County in 1829, he had inherited a ranch of close to one million acres. He had attended universities in St. Louis and New York, had been a college professor of the classics, had practiced law in New York and Albuquerque, and had been elected to three successive terms as New Mexico's delegate to the Congress in the critical era preceding the Civil War.

After the war the building of the Santa Fe Railroad westward had created an opportunity for the marketing of wares shipped by rail. Otero formed a partnership with J.P. Sellar and opened a store at the temporary end of the track in three towns in succession in Colorado and at Otero and Las Vegas in New Mexico. In the latter place, which then was booming, the partners sold out to the Gross, Blackwell Company, and Otero founded a bank, organized the first telephone company in the territory, and invested in mines and real estate, prior to his succumbing to pneumonia in 1882.

His sons, who had been born in St. Louis, remained there for their education while their father was moving westward, and then the family settled in Las Vegas in 1879. Part of the deal when he disposed of the mercantile business was that the new owners should employ Miguel, Jr., then only 20 years old, in an executive position in that business. Daniel Kelly, son of a later partner, wrote afterward that the employing of that "playboy" in a responsible position did not at first inspire much confidence in the business community.

While in that employment and later as a cashier in a local bank, Miguel A., Jr., familiarly called "Gillie," did have a good time while also rendering community services. He was a member of the first volunteer fire company, he was one of the leaders of the vigilantes, he and his brother Page played on the local semi-pro baseball team, he was active in political campaigns, he joined the exclusive Montezuma Club, all Anglos but him, which maintained luxurious club rooms, and he became a charter member of the first Elks Club founded in New Mexico.

Miguel A. Otero, Jr., of Las Vegas was a popular, appointed governor of the territory for nine years (Museum of New Mexico).

Once when a committee of ladies was appointed by the Board of Trade to prepare an exhibit for the advertising of the products of Las Vegas, they had it crowned by a bust of "Gillie," because, they said, he was a "typical Spanish American." Actually he was not typical, because he was not a native of New Mexico, his associates were the sons of Anglo merchants and bankers, and he married a girl from Minnesota in an Episcopal ceremony.

Certainly he was a popular citizen who in his maturity was showing evidences of sobriety and responsibility. The upshot was that a local influential banker, Jefferson Raynolds, who had contacts in Washington, was said to have been the one who pressed for the appointment of Otero as territorial governor, and President William McKinley responded favorably in 1897.

Recently an eminent historian, Howard R. Lamar, wrote that the appointment of Otero, a Spanish American, effected a "revolution" in New Mexico politics, but that revolution was little more than in name only. Otero did originate the idea of having a regiment enlisted in the Southwest for action in the war with Spain in 1898, and he did contribute progress toward the achievement of statehood for New Mexico in 1912, beyond the end of his term in office. Also, he did respond with intervention in behalf of Hispanos whenever the opportunity arose, but he did not press for measures which for them would promise great economic and social advancement. Republican railroad, land, and statehood politics continued to prevail.

The principal revolution which occurred during Otero's regime was the livening up of the capital by the conducting of brilliant balls, receptions, and banquets. One might anticipate that there would be a swarming of *dons* in attendance, but that was not the case, as the published lists of participants included the usual run of prominent Republican politicians and business magnates.

Otero's chief complaint was that a rival Republican, Thomas B. Catron, head of the Santa Fe Ring of landgrabbers, was eternally trying to undermine him and thwart his recommended appointments. This could have been expected, because he had tangled with Catron previously. After Otero's father had died, he found that he had inherited title to a mine near Santa Fe; but Catron, by expanding the boundaries of a land grant which he had acquired, laid claim to that mine and had men there working in it. Gillie and his brother then had enlisted some friends, had forcefully run out Catron's miners, and had holed up in that mine themselves until

67

the sheriff of Santa Fe County arrested Gillie and jailed him. Rather than to give bail and have a trial before a pro-Ring judge, Otero had remained in jail until friends from Las Vegas had broken him out. Thus this future governor, like Donaciano Vigil before him, had spent several weeks in the lockup in Santa Fe. Needless to say, Otero and Catron would be antagonists thenceforth.

Although Otero was not the first Hispano to be appointed as governor, because Donaciano Vigil had that distinction, that had been a long time before, in 1847, so that certainly the citizens of Spanish descent had reason to be pleased that they had a representative in that high office after so long a recess. Further, although Otero was thoroughly anglicized, he did definitely bring an Hispanic name and aura into that eminent position, and his tactful, responsible, popular administration did redound with credit to the Spanish-American people, especially in some circles in the East where previously they had not been held in high regard.

XXII Some Founding Fathers

The story, often told, about how New Mexico once lost statehood by a handshake, will bear repeating. Ever since the American occupation, bills had been introduced in Congress, and conventions had been held in this territory, in an effort to gain admission to the Union. Finally in 1876 it appeared that New Mexico had a good opportunity to be accepted along with Colorado. When Stephen B. Elkins, New Mexico's delegate, was lobbying for it, once as he heard a congressman from the North being applauded just as he had finished a speech, he rushed in to shake his hand in congratulations. It happened that that speech had been one, typical of that era, waving "the bloody shirt" of the Civil War by blaming the South for having tried to destroy the Union. The Southern congressmen who saw Elkins congratulate the speaker then turned against New Mexico and helped vote in only Colorado.

Opposition to statehood was not expressed alone by a faction in the East but also by several men of prominence in New Mexico, who feared that it would cause higher taxes and who did not favor giving a share in government to the "Mexicans." In 1890, when it appeared that New Mexico had a chance again, Governor L. Bradford Prince took a special railway carload of prominent men to Washington to lobby for that and some other causes; but on the way there they fell into a dispute over statehood, with the result that upon their arrival they pressed for other legislation and did nothing about statehood.

As the debate in the East waxed warmer, literate New Mexicans became infuriated, and bombarded Washington with resolutions in protest, when the opponents of statehood described them as "violent, immoral, unamericanized greasers," who were "ignorant, superstitious, and dominated by the priests." Then the 400 of Theodore Roosevelt's Rough Riders from this territory won his friendship, so that while he was president after 1901, he favored statehood. However, the best that the pros and cons in Washington could come up with then was a compromise act proposing that New Mexico and Arizona be admitted as one state. Most New Mexicans were opposed, but they had been frustrated for so long that a majority voted for it. However, this plan, called "jointure," was voted down in Arizona.

As the year 1910 was approaching, conditions in the Territory of

New Mexico grew more favorable. The population was increasing past 300,000, and headway was being made in suppressing outlawry, clearing land titles, and strengthening public education. This territory, and Arizona, too, could not be held back much longer; therefore the Congress in 1910 finally adopted a resolution enabling both to prepare for admission as states.

When 100 delegates were elected in 1910 as members of the convention to draft a constitution, thirty-two of them were prominent Spanish Americans, who were listed as follows by Ralph Emerson Twitchell: Bernalillo County, A.A. Sedillo, Anastacio Gutiérrez, and Nestor Montoya; Colfax County, Francisco Guana; Doña Ana County, Isidoro Armijo; Guadalupe County, Salome Martínez and Tranquilino Labadie; Lincoln County, Jacobo Aragón; Mora County, E.M. Lucero, Anastacio Medina, and Juan Navarro; Rio Arriba County, Vencenlado Jaramillo, Perfecto Esquibel, and José A. Lucero; Sandoval County, José D. Sena and Victor Ortega; San Miguel County, Margarito Romero, Atanasio Roibal, Luciano Maes, Eugenio Romero, and Nepomuceno Segura; Santa Fe County, José D. Sena and Victor Ortega; Socorro Coun-

Thirty-two Hispanos participated in the deliberations of the State Constitutional convention in 1910 (Museum of New Mexico; photo by William R. Walton).

ty, A.C. Abeytia and J. Frank Romero; Taos County, Malaquias Martínez and Onésimo Martínez, Torrance County, Acasio Gallegos; Union County, Eufracio Gallegos and Candelario Vigil; and Valencia County, Solomón Luna and Sylvestre Miraval.

The gathering of so many Hispanos elicited a remark in a New York newspaper, as quoted by Victor Westphall, that this was a constitutional convention and not "some bull fight in a Mexican village." Unperturbed, the delegates set up a central committee headed by the Hispanic sage, Solomón Luna, which did most of the work. Since 71 of the men were Republicans, the product was a relatively conservative document.

When it was submitted to the electorate for approval, opponents pointed out that the constitution was difficult to amend, that it lacked provisions for initiative and referendum, that it did not give women the franchise in school elections, that it created a legislature larger than needed, and that it provided for salaries higher that the taxpayers could afford. Nevertheless, the voters adopted it by a large majority, perhaps as some observers thought, because they were voting for statehood, at last, more than they were for the constitution.

The eminent Hispanos who had shared in its making must have been greatly gratified, after they had been so vilely slandered, when the Congress approved the constitution of New Mexico, whereas President Howard Taft found a flaw in that of Arizona, which he requested that they eliminate. That delayed the process there so that New Mexico was admitted alone in 1911 as the 47th state, for which the new government was launched in 1912.

XXIII   First but Frustrated

From 1889 to 1892 a rural rebellion caused turmoil in Las Vegas and vicinity. Villagers, called *Las Gorras Blancas*, because they wore white hoods, cut fences, burned haystacks, destroyed thousands of freshly cut railroad ties, and made frightening demonstrations in town. Sheriff's deputies were unable to stop the depredations, grand juries failed to get convincing evidence on anyone, and the governor appealed in vain for a cessation.

Since no authoritative management of the Las Vegas Land Grant had been established as yet, ranchers were buying up the imaginary shares of claims of the heirs of original settlers to the unoccupied lands and were fencing grasslands upon which villagers had been grazing their sheep. In addition, *dons* were maintaining camps of workmen who were stripping the mountains of timber for cutting into ties for sale to railroads. Simultaneously a Republican political "machine" headed by the wealthy Romeros and their affiliated *dons*, lawyers, merchants, and bankers maintained a stifling control of county offices. The causes of the uprising, therefore, were attributed about half and half to "landgrabbing" and "Republican oppression."

Coincidental with the beginning of the rebellion was the launching of a local Spanish-language newspaper, *La Voz del Pueblo*, by Félix Martínez, who either inspired the uprising or at least encouraged it by editorial defense of the participants and ferocious criticism of the Republican *políticos*. As a new party, The People's Party, or "Populists," was being launched, that newspaper supported it, too. Simultaneously, whenever Juan José Herrera organized local units of a new, radical union, the Knights of Labor, fence cutting began in those localities. This suggested that Herrera was the leader of the White Caps, who secretly were the members of that labor union; but he denied it, and *La Voz* defended the Knights as standing for "high principles."

In the midst of this turmoil Ezekiel C. de Baca joined the staff of *La Voz del Pueblo*. He was a great grandson of Luis María C. de Baca, the wealthy, prolific *don* who has been introduced early in this series, and his father, Tomás, was an influential citizen of Las Vegas before he moved to La Liendre. Ezekiel was born in 1864, before that move was made. He received his higher education in the college maintained by Jesuits in Las Vegas from 1877 to 1888. For a

Ezekiel C. de Baca of Las Vegas was the first Hispano to be elected as governor of the state (Museum of New Mexico).

while he tried various occupations, including two years as a teacher in a rural school, before he became a journalist in 1891. Then this descendant of aristocrats fell right in with the policy of *La Voz del Pueblo* in the campaign in behalf of the common man.

When the rural rebellion subsided in 1892, all it had accomplished was the election of several Populists to county offices and to the legislature. Eminent among them was the publisher, Félix Martínez, whose support of the uprising had helped him win election to the Council (the equivalent of a Senate). There he was influential in getting Las Vegas chosen as the site for a normal university in 1893.

As the White Caps lapsed into inactivity, and as Populism declined, *La Voz* became a Democratic paper in opposition to the Republican *Daily Optic*. Then its editor, Antonio Lucero, and his associate, Don Ezekiel, took up as their causes the recognition of Hispanic contributions, the need for bilingual education, and alleged abuses by the Land Grant Board which was appointed in 1902. C. de Baca's biographer, Anselmo Arellano, by studying mainly the writings of his subject, concluded that he had a "strong determination to represent his people and help them achieve a more meaningful status...." Circumstances required that that objective be supplemented by another, to break the power of the Republican bosses by helping Democrats win election. That required, in turn, that he, like Féliz Martínez and Antonio Lucero, become a skillful agitator who could raise issues which would incite rural men and workingmen to change their voting habits. In consequence, although he never had held a local office, and conveyed the impression that he never had sought one, the county Democrats advanced his candidacy for a high office, that of governor when New Mexico was being admitted as a state.

The state convention, however, nominated W.C. McDonald and chose C. de Baca for his running mate, with Antonio Lucero also on the ticket as their candidate for election as secretary of state. Lucero then was a member of the faculty of the Normal University. Ordinarily the Republicans would have won, but nationally at that time that party was being split by a Progressive movement, and it caused a schism in Republican ranks in New Mexico, too. This enabled the Democrats to win several offices. McDonald surprisingly defeated Solomón Luna's protegé, Holm O. Bursum, and carried into office with him C. de Baca and Lucero. During McDonald's administration Don Ezekiel as lieutenant governor exerted his influence in attempts to get Spanish taught in all public schools and all teachers trained to be bilingual. By holding himself aloof from major conflicts, he enhanced his popularity, so that, without his overtly seeking it, the Democrats nominated him as their candidate for election as governor in 1916, to run against Holm O. Bursum.

C. de Baca launched a vigorous campaign, which elicited an enthusiastic response wherever he went, but toward the end he became ill and had to cancel some engagements. Nevertheless, he won. By January he was so ill that he could not attend his inauguration, and after a month in which he never was able to function as governor, he died on February 18, 1917.

What he might have accomplished can be only a matter of conjecture, but probably not much in the pursuit of his objectives, due to the entry of the United States into World War I. His objectives were economic and social, and the crisis of the war set back other such programs by requiring that all resources be mustered in the drive to victory. Although frustrated by his illness, Ezekiel C. de Baca did have the satisfaction of being the first Hispano to be elected by the people, not appointed, as governor of New Mexico.

XXIV   The Emergence of Women

Back in the Mexican Period women enjoyed much freedom. They could have paid employment, could own property, could sue in the courts, and, on the other hand, could be put in jail. They had the privilege of participating in pleasurable activities even on Sundays, and they dabbed on rouge, seldom hid their faces behind a veil, and wore short dresses, much in contrast to the well-covered women of the States in that era.

Besides presenting abundant evidence of those liberties, Janet Lecompte in an article in *The Western Historical Quarterly* went on to explain how the Hispanic women became subdued after the American occupation. The change resulted from the imposition of the masculine ego by soldiers and frontiersmen, the restriction of rights by American courts, and the banning of amusements on Sundays by the French priests brought in by Bishop Lamy. By 1900 they and the Anglo women had come to be regarded in the main as belonging in the home.

Immediately after New Mexico had achieved statehood, a strong feminist movement arose, and it gathered impetus as women took jobs which contributed to the all-out effort for victory in World War I. In New Mexico resistance was entrenched. During the Constitutional Convention in 1910 Solomón Luna had favored the granting of the franchise to women in school elections, but the patriarchal tradition of a majority of the delegates prevailed. It was fostered, too, by a powerful Republican, Thomas B. Catron, who would be a hard nut to crack, because he was known to have openly expressed the conviction that the role of women was to raise children and to do housework.

As suffragists from outside sought to change the prevailing attitude in this state, they enlisted a few Anglo workers and then made a special effort to gain Hispanic collaborators. They did, and prominent among them by 1915 were three nieces of the aforementioned Solomón Luna.

The nationwide organization, called "The Congressional Union," needed a chairwoman in New Mexico. For that job a visiting representative in 1917 obtained acceptance by one of those nieces, Mrs. Adelina Otero-Warren, a widow at the relatively youthful age of 34.

At first, according to Jean M. Jensen, writing in *the New Mexico*

Nina Otero Warren.

Historical Review, Señora Otero-Warren was very shy about speaking in public, but soon she overcame that reticence. She had a special advantage in that she had influential male relatives among the Oteros and Lunas, whom she had a fair chance to convert, and then they could sway others.

As Mrs. Otero-Warren was launching a campaign for the organizing of workers, who would emerge in lobbying and in the distribuiting of leaflets in Spanish, she was appointed school superintendent in Santa Fe in 1917 and then set a precedent for other women by winning that positon by election the following year.

The first task, to get the suffrage amendment to the Constitution of the United States through Congress, required that she join with others for lobbying in Washington, which met with success. Next, to obtain ratification by the legislature in New Mexico she and co-workers appealed individually to the members of the House of Representatives and easily won the approval of that body. The Senate would be more difficult, but she managed to gain admission to the Republican caucus, as the first woman ever to attend one of those meetings, and her persuasive appeal did the trick; the Senate approved ratification of the amendment in 1920 by a vote of seventeen to five. Nationwide adoption finally gave the franchise to women.

Next, when a few ladies began trying for election to public offices, Mrs. Otero-Warren ran as a candidate for the House of Representatives in 1922. If she had won, she would have been the first Hispanic woman to have that distinction. However, she lost, but another woman, an Anglo, did win election in that year, and a Hispanic lady won election as Superintendent of Public Instruction. Others kept trying, but with limited success, so that by 1931 there were only three women in the House and one in the Senate. Significantly, among the three in the House were Mrs. P. Sáiz of Socorro and Mrs. Ezekiel Gallegos of Wagon Mound.

Subsequently the emergence of many women of diverse heritages in many types of community work and in city, county, and state offices in New Mexico owed its origin in a large measure to the skillful and courageous endeavors of that persuasive suffragist, Mrs. Otero-Warren, during the early years of statehood.

XXV   The Outspoken Governor

Those who had known Octaviano A. Larrazolo, or had heard him make a speech, remembered him well. They had been impressed by that man, who was suave in manner, distinguished in appearance, and strong in personality. Moreover, he made such brilliant, provocative speeches that he acquired the reputation of being the greatest orator in New Mexico in his time, in both Spanish and English.

Although he addressed his appeal to fellow Hispanos, he was not a native of New Mexico, as he had been born in Allende, Mexico, in 1859. However, he did cross the border into Texas quite early, at the age of eleven. At San Elizario, Texas, a traveling clergyman, the Rt. Rev. J. B. Salpointe, Vicar of Arizona, met that bright, orphaned boy, practically adopted him, and took him back to Arizona.

Salpointe saw to it that Octaviano got good schooling, and when he was transferred to Santa Fe in 1884, he was accompanied by his protegé, who enrolled in St. Michael's college. There Larrazolo excelled in his studies and cultivated his talent as an orator in collegiate debating contests.

After teaching one year in a school in Tucsón, he returned to San Elizario for a tenure there of six years as school principal. As he had meanwhile become politically active in the Democratic Party, next he won election as a district court clerk, studied law on the side, and gained admission to the Texas Bar.

In 1895 Larrazolo was attracted to the lively town of Las Vegas, New Mexico, where he opened a law office and began making many friends, including another future governor, Ezekiel C. de Baca. Soon he went into politics again, but not as a candidate for local offices. Instead, he set his sights on the highest territorial office then filled by vote of the electorate, that of delegate to the Congress of the United States.

Thrice he won the Democratic nomination for that office, and, according to his biographer, Paul A. F. Walter, he based his campaigns on "fiery and persistent pleas for race consciousness addressed to the Spanish-speaking people"; but all three times he failed to crack the solid control of voters by the Republican politicians. The third time, in 1908, when it appeared that he was about to beat W. H. "Bull" Andrews, investigative reporting by the Republican *Las Vegas Daily Optic* cost him some votes. That paper headlined

Octaviano A. Larrazolo of Las Vegas was the first Hispano to be elected to the United States Senate (Museum of New Mexico).

allegations that Larrazolo had not paid his county taxes, amounting to $874.91, and that in Mora County, too, he was a "tax dodger" who owed $1,097.35. After he had lost, a man in Albuquerque wrote in a letter to the newspaper that there his efforts "to raise race prejudice" caused them to resent "the attitude of a foreigner who had come among them and attempted to prove that he is a better American than they are."

This was not a case of a Hispano trying to break into a select office from which they had been excluded, because from 1849 to 1900 of the 16 men who had been elected as delegates, nine had been Spanish Americans. Instead, it was a case of a Democrat trying desperately to align all Hispanos on his side by arousing antagonisms which might help him win.

Finally, in 1911, when New Mexico was preparing to elect the first state governor, Larrazolo switched his affiliation to the Republican Party, because, he said, he could "do more for the people in that party." Actually, one reason causing him to bolt from the Democratic Party was that the state convention had rejected his demand that statewide one-half of all nominees should be Hispanos. Statistics were on his side, because at that time people of Spanish descent comprised 60 percent of the population of the state.

As lines were being drawn for the campaign in 1911, the Republican politicians in Las Vegas did not greet Larrazolo's entry into their ranks with great enthusiasm. They let him sit on the sidelines and advanced for their choice as governor their acknowledged "boss," Secundino Romero, who got the nomination for election as lieutenant governor. However, as related previously, a surprising Democratic victory carried into that office Larrazolo's erstwhile co-worker, Ezekiel C. de Baca.

As Larrazolo was being held back, he became even more fervent in his "racial" contentions, so that the Republicans were not "digesting" him well; yet he did storm his way into nomination for election as governor in 1918. Then, when Republicans were coming back into favor again, he won, and by all accounts he handled well the duties of that office, except that he did incur much criticism by calling out the National Guard to suppress a strike by miners in 1919. Otherwise he got credit for setting up the Child Welfare Board and the State Health Board, for advancing tax reforms, for seeking federal aid for farmers during a severe drought, and for contending that federal lands should be ceded to the state.

80

Meanwhile, to quote Walter again, his outspoken appeal for "racial" alignment almost "rent the Republican Party asunder." After his term as governor they set him aside for six years, and finally, in 1928, he became their nominee to run as a candidate for election to the United States Senate. Partly with the aid of a Republican victory in the nation, he succeeded in becoming the first Hispano ever to enter into that august assemblage. There his colleagues expressed surprise that that "Mexican" could speak English so fluently. Soon, however, his effectiveness was hampered by an illness which brought his life to an end in 1930.

Certainly, despite the criticism which the outspoken O. A. Larrazolo had engendered, he had earned for himself a place of great eminence in the early history of the State of New Mexico.

XXVI   Leading Ladies

Thus far biographies of women have been scarce in these pages, because this review had been dealing with an era in which, with a few exceptions, they had not surfaced into the public limelight. For most of them their wholesome role in their communities had been limited to the influence they had on their husbands and the work they did in their church societies.

Finally, in the 1920s, after women had won the right to vote and had become liberated from other restraints, several emerged as leaders in their communities and even in state and national affairs. For the two Hispanic ladies selected here as pacemakers, there was no shooting, no scandal, no strife to liven up these sketches, like for some of the earlier subjects in this series; instead, their stories are simply records of remarkable achievements.

The first, and the elder of the two, Fabiola Cabeza de Baca Gilbert, born in 1898, had been essentially rural in her orientation. She received her B.S. degree in Home Economics from New Mexico State University in 1929, after having been graduated first from New Mexico Normal University in Las Vegas, and then, as described by her biographer, Nancy Benson, she was employed for 30 years as a Cooperative Extension Service Agent in northern rural areas in this state, where she taught home-making skills.

To facilitate her work, she wrote bulletins in Spanish on food preparation, nutrition, methods of canning, and use of the sewing machine. She also developed new recipes for use of pinto beans and chili peppers and explained how better to prepare dyes and medicines from native plants. Next, by learning the Tiwa and Tewa languages, she became the first agent to extend the work among the women of the Indian pueblos.

Further, in 1951 the United Nations sent her to Mexico to establish demonstration centers among the Tarascan Indians, and afterward she drew upon that experience for assisting with training programs for Peace Corps volunteers.

Somehow along the way Mrs. Gilbert found time to turn out two popular books, *The Good Life* in 1949 and *We Fed Them Cactus* in 1954, which, as Benson put it, "recorded the traditions, customs, and daily life of her Spanish ancestors who pioneered New Mexico."

The other distinguished subject, Concha Ortiz y Pino de Kleven, born in 1914, has been more urban in the later aspects of her

Fabiola Cabeza de Baca Gilbert

associations. First, in the early 1930s she promoted the founding of a vocational school in Galisteo for reviving the crafts of dyeing, spinning, weaving, and leather work and for improving the local economy in other ways.

When she was elected to the New Mexico House of Representatives in 1936, she was not quite the first Hispanic lady to win that distinction, but one of the early few, and certainly in her three terms in Santa Fe she was one of the more energetic of all representatives, male and female. She sponsored legislation for bilingual education, for women to serve on juries, and for establishing the School of Inter-American Affairs at the University of New Mexico. Moreover, she became the only woman ever to hold the position as "whip" of the majority party.

Her other activites were wide in scope. She pressed for laws to remove barriers to the handicapped in public buildings, originated Project Newgate for rehabilitation of men serving terms in the penitentiary, became a member of the National Council of the Upward Bound Program, organized the New Mexico Arts Commission, and served on the boards of the National Council on the Humanities and the National Council of Christians and Jews.

As summed up by Nancy Benson, who is her biographer, too, Mrs. Pino de Kleven "has served in official and volunteer capacities in a wide range of organizations and institutions from the local to the national level."

These two sketches have presented trailblazers for the many Hispanic ladies who have become eminent on their public services in the Land of Enchantment in this century.

XXVII The Political "Godfather"

An agricultural depression in the United States in the 1920s hit hard in New Mexico, where in some areas it was also aggravated by a severe drought. Then in the 1930s during the Great Depression conditions became even worse. Banks closed, businesses failed, ranchers became impoverished, workers lost their jobs, and many families became destitute.

To that time the prevailing theory had maintained that the economy functioned best if government left it alone, except for a necessary minimum of policing, and that a government, like any business, should have a balanced budget. Spurred on by desperate needs during the Depression, the new Democratic administration of Franklin Delano Roosevelt departed from the previous theory. He commanded the support of the Congress for the enactment of a series of laws, called "The New Deal," by which the federal government undertook direct relief for the needy, adopted measures to create jobs and to aid and control business, and enacted laws to foster future security. That "revolution" also included adoption of a new economic theory which held that government is not like a private business; instead it would be wholesome for the federal government to run up indebtedness in order to keep the economy stable by fluctuating the rate of borrowing and spending and by controlling interest rates.

In the late 1920s, when conditions were becoming bad, Dionisio "Dennis" Chávez was entering politics. He had been born in Los Chávez in 1888 of the same illustrious lineage as that of Amado Chaves, the first territorial school superintendent, that is, having an ancestry traceable back to Fernando Durán y Chaves, who had arrived in New Mexico in 1693.

Dennis was employed by the city government of Albuquerque from 1907 to 1916, followed by work with a contracting firm. Then Senator Andreius A. Jones obtained employment for him in Washington so that he could attend law school at night. As pointed out by Maurilio E. Vigil, one of his biographers, that was the beginning of a practice whereby scores of young men from this state were able to earn an education in Washington as subsequent protegés of Chávez and other congressmen from New Mexico. Dennis was graduated from the law school of Georgetown University in 1926, opened a law office in Albuquerque, and after a term in the

U.S. Senator Dennis Chavez.

state legislature he launched a campaign for election to the United
States House of Representatives in 1930, as a Democrat.

To that time a majority of the Spanish Americans had been
Republican, but when they became destitute, and then received
benefits from the programs of the New Deal, they became inclined
to switch their party affiliation. Tibo V. Chávez wrote that by
swinging those voters over to the Democratic Party, Dennis Chávez
broke the power of the Oteros and Lunas of Valencia County. It

could be said, too, that first the hard times and then the New Deal caused them to begin swinging over, and that Chávez was astute in his choice of the party which would be gaining voters and would give him an opportunity better to serve people in need.

Meanwhile another trend had become significant. As the population of the state had grown, the proportion of the people who were Hispanos had declined from 57 percent in 1915 until it would become only 37 percent by 1950. No longer could a politician hope to win statewide by pleading solely for solidarity of the Hispanos, as O. A. Larrazolo had done. Instead, one had to seek the support of other Democrats, too, especially of those former Texans who had migrated into the eastern part of New Mexico. The uniting of those two blocs required great skill, because the outcome of influences upon the voting of the Spanish Americans in the northern counties was hard to predict. After attempting to analyze it, Jack Holmes concluded that it was a "baffling endeavor."

Whatever it took, Dennis Chávez had it. He won election to the House and won reelection, and when Senator Bronson Cutting, another New Dealer, was killed in an airplane crash in 1935, the governor appointed Chávez to fill the remainder of his term. Afterward he was elected to the Senate and reelected until finally in 1962 he died while still holding that office. In that time, besides taking a special interest in fair employment practices, in the development of western resources, and in improvement of relations with Latin America, he gave much attention to the needs of the Spanish Americans in his home state. Thus it came about that many who had shared in his dispensation of New Deal benefits had almost a worshipful high regard for their chief benefactor.

When New Mexico was invited to select a most distinguished citizen for the placing of a statue of him in Statuary Hall in the Capitol in Washingtion, the members of the New Mexico Historical Society chose Dennis Chávez.

XXVIII   New Ways in the New World

Soon after the opening of the New World the people of northern Europe, previously engaged essentially in agriculture and commerce, became animated by revolutionary movements emphasizing industrialization and democratization, which presently overwhelmed the previous medieval pattern of life there. To America the English settlers transplanted those achievements and added contributions in public education, religious freedom, improved transportation, and scientific investigation.

As the innovations spread elsewhere, advocates emerged in southern Europe too, but there the deficiency in resources for industrial development and the resistance of strong vested interests delayed the transformation. The major components of society continued to be the land-owning, governing aristocrats, the peasants, slaves, soldiers, and priests, and the freemen in the towns. In consequence, the leaders in the colonization of Hispanic America transplanted to it that medieval pattern still prevalent in southern Europe, and that pattern was carried by colonists to the northern frontier of New Spain.

Nevertheless, proponents of industrialization, democracy, and public education emerged in the Hispanic colonies, including Mexico, and there they kept trying; but, as in Spain, the transformation which finally occurred was delayed by a long revolutionary struggle.

On the other hand, in the area incorporated within the United States in 1846, many Hispanos found themselves residing in a nation already being transformed. This opened up for them an opportunity to demonstrate their capacities for leadership in government, commerce, agriculture, education, science, and the arts. That opportunity was immediate for those already having the advantage of an advanced education, which in the beginning was an attribute limited mostly to *dons*, priests, and sons of *dons*. As facilities for education became available to others, the circle widened.

In these profiles before 1846 the earlier influences prevailed, that is, essentially medieval relationships, amid which a few sought greater freedom and some became interested in commercial development. After that date many of the Hispanos, as represented by those in this series, contributed much to the ascendency of the new pattern of institutions and strove successfully to gain education, wealth, and prestige within it, while others labored to improve conditions which had crept in as by-products of the transformation.

Today Hispanos are continuing their prominence in both roles not only in New Mexico but also throughout the Southwest and Latin America.

The word "historical" had been inserted in the title of this series to indicate that it omits recent politicians and living persons, whose contributions can be evaluated better after they have been allowed to jell for a generation. However, in order to introduce the vanguard of the emerging crop of feminine leaders, a slight inconsistency has been injected by the inclusion of two who are still living at the time of writing. In addition, the span of the service of Senator Chávez continued to a relatively recent date, but this work could not well be terminated without including that late senator who had been selected for memorializing in Statuary Hall as the state's most distinguished citizen.

INDEX

90

PHOTO INDEX

The following photographs, listed with their file numbers, their photographers, and in order of their appearance in the book are courtesy of the MUSEUM OF NEW MEXICO: